ULTIMATE
Chocolate

ULTIMATE
Chocolate

PATRICIA LOUSADA

Food styling by Janice Murfitt

Photography by Ian O'Leary

DORLING KINDERSLEY
London • New York • Sydney • Moscow

A Dorling Kindersley Book

Art Editor Jane Bull
Editor Janice Anderson
Assistant Editor Lorraine Turner
DTP Designer Bridget Roseberry
Managing Editors Fay Franklin
Mary Ling
Deputy Art Director Carole Ash
Production Manager Maryann Rogers

First published in Great Britain in 1997
by Dorling Kindersley Limited,
9 Henrietta Street, London WC2E 8PS
Visit us on the World Wide Web
at http://www.dk.com

A CIP catalogue for this book is available
from the British Library

ISBN 0 7513 0369 0

Reproduced by Colourscan, Singapore
Printed and bound by Graphicom (Italy)

Contents

Introduction

Chocolate is one of the world's most delectable foods and the one that most satisfies our desire for something sweet. Its special rich flavour can create the most delicious cakes, biscuits, ice creams and other desserts and even savoury recipes. When we think of a treat to please we think of chocolate.

Where Chocolate Comes From

Chocolate is made from the bean of a tree, *Theobroma cacao*, native to the tropical areas of Central and South America. Thousands of years before it arrived in Europe the Maya and Aztecs were brewing it as a drink, offering it to their gods during tribal rituals and using it for currency. The Aztec emperors kept vast storehouses of cocoa beans, which they used as treasuries.

When Columbus returned from the New World in 1502, bringing cocoa beans for the King of Spain, no one showed much interest in them. Twenty years later, after conquering Mexico, Cortez also brought cocoa to Spain. He had first tasted it at the Mexican court of Montezuma in a cold, bitter drink called xocolatl ("bitter water"). This was made with chillies and other native flavourings and was topped with a foamy froth created by the cocoa butter.

South American Indian with chocolate pot and cup

In Mexico, the Spanish conquistadores adopted the Aztecs' practice of using the cocoa beans for wage and market transactions, but it took longer for them to get accustomed to the bitter drink.

Over time, thanks to intermarriages between the two cultures, the unpalatably bitter drink evolved. It was sweetened with sugar, flavoured with Old World spices such as cinnamon and anise, and served hot. Another refinement was the *molinillo*, a wooden swizzle-stick used to whip the cocoa into a froth. The Aztecs had favoured a method of pouring the drink from one vessel to another to create the foam.

Europe Discovers Chocolate

In this new form, cocoa was successfully introduced into Spain. It was a drink for the elite, who took to it for its medicinal effects as well as for its taste. Over time, the new drink's popularity spread. Missionaries who had been to South America brought it back to monasteries and convents in Italy and south-west France. It trickled into court life through the intermarriage of royal families. In 1660 the Infanta Maria Theresa of Spain married the King of France, Louis XIV. She and her retinue were fond of chocolate, and the personal maid who prepared it was nicknamed "la Molina" by the French court. Within ten years, chocolate was well established at Versailles and throughout French aristocratic and intellectual circles.

A noble French family takes chocolate

We can get an idea of how splendidly it was served from Mme D'Aulnoy, a French visitor to the court of Spain. In 1679 she wrote:

"They presented next Chocolate, each cup of porcelain on a saucer of agate garnished with gold, with the sugar in a bowl of the same. There was iced chocolate, another hot and another with Milk and Eggs, one took it with a Biscuit, or rather with dry small buns...."

For two and a half centuries, controversy raged within Catholic countries as to whether the taking of chocolate broke the ecclesiastical fast. Was it food to nourish the body or a beverage to quench thirst? The Jesuits, who traded in chocolate, held it did not break the fast; the Dominicans took the opposite view.

When chocolate appeared in England in the middle of the seventeenth century, chocolate houses became important meeting places for the fashionable and well-to-do. Samuel Pepys wrote in his Diary of enjoying "jocalatte" and writers like Addison and Steele mention the chocolate houses in their works. The drink was an expensive luxury, so heavily taxed by the government that cocoa beans were often smuggled into the country. When Gladstone lowered the chocolate tax in 1853, prices fell and even the less affluent could now enjoy chocolate.

English covered chocolate cup, c.1805

Drinking Chocolate Becomes Eating Chocolate

Until 1828 cocoa for drinking was manufactured by grinding the beans into a "chocolate liquor" and adding spices and sugar, as well as some kind of farinaceous substance to soak up the cocoa butter which tended to float to the top. A major breakthrough occurred in that year when the Dutch chemist Coenraad J. Van Houten invented a press to extract cocoa butter from the bean, leaving a dry cake that could be ground into an almost fat-free cocoa powder similar to that of today. Van Houten's press was used in England by the leading chocolate manufacturers of the day. Two of these companies were owned by prominent Quaker families, Cadbury and Fry. It was they who, twenty years later and as a direct result of this innovation, produced the first eating chocolate.

In the United States, too, the early cocoa manufacturers are still among today's leaders. In 1765, Dr. James Baker joined forces with a newly arrived Irish cocoa-maker and started the now famous Walter Baker company. Domenico Ghirardelli, drawn to California by the gold rush, opened a chocolate factory in San Francisco in 1849. It continues to produce chocolate and the landmark buildings that once housed its company are known as Ghirardelli Square. Hershey, too, is a household name; Milton S. Hershey founded a whole town in Pennsylvania as a result of his chocolate success. Like something out of a child's fantasy, Hershey, Pennsylvania, has streets named Cocoa and Chocolate Avenue, and lampposts shaped after his famous "kisses".

How Chocolate is Made

As the world's appetite for chocolate increased — and it is still increasing today — manufacturing methods improved to meet the growing demand. Turning cocoa beans into edible chocolate is a long and complicated process. It begins, of course, on the plantations, which are always located within twenty degrees of the equator. Even at this latitude the trees will not be productive if the altitude is too high or the temperature falls below 16°C. They also require a rain forest atmosphere

Cocoa pod and beans

where midges thrive, as they are the only insects that pollinate the small five-petalled flowers. Cocoa trees start producing their fruit when they are four to five years old. The beans, or seeds, grow in spindle-shaped pods that form on the trunk and thickest branches of the tree. The pods are harvested twice a year and split open at once with a machete, so the beans can be scooped out and left to dry in the sun. An average tree yields only one or two pounds of dried beans a year, since the beans lose 50 per cent of their weight during drying. There are two main varieties of beans: the Forastero, a high-yielding bean which provides 80 per cent of the world's cacao crop and the Criollo, a superior-flavoured bean that is often blended with the Forastero to improve its flavour. There are also a number of hybrid beans, of which the Trinitario is the best known. Each manufacturer processes its own beans using a personal formula. The overall process, however, is the same throughout the world. The beans are roasted to bring out their flavour and then cracked so their protective shells and husks can be removed, leaving the kernels, called nibs. Once these have been exposed they must be ground. The friction of the grinding melts the cocoa butter in the nibs and extracts most of it, leaving a thick paste called "chocolate liquor". This liquor, cooled and hardened, is unsweetened cooking chocolate. If the liquor is then pressed, more cocoa butter will be released from it, and the remaining hard mass, ground to powder, becomes cocoa.

All chocolate liquor retains some of its original cocoa butter content. To form sweetened chocolate, extra cocoa butter is added to the liquor along with sugar and flavourings, such as vanilla. Milk chocolate, now made with dried milk, was originally created in 1875 using condensed milk. We owe the smooth texture of chocolate as we now know it to a Swiss manufacturer named Rodolphe Lindt, who invented "conching". Until 1880, all eating chocolate had a rough, grainy texture. Lindt increased the amount of cocoa butter in his chocolate recipes. In his conch-shaped machine the enriched liquor was blended repeatedly over several days — much longer than was customary. The result of this innovation was the smooth, creamy chocolate we know today.

Advertisement for chocolate, 1913

Chocolate and Good Health

The effects of chocolate on health have long been debated. Too much sugar, we know, is not good for us. A fine quality dark chocolate has only a small amount of sugar and a large amount of nutrients, such as calcium, potassium, riboflavin, niacin, and vitamin A. Recent research has found that chocolate's high level of phenol is helpful against heart disease. As for keeping us awake, compared to the 75–175 milligrams of caffeine in a cup of coffee, cocoa has a meagre 25 milligrams to none at all.

Chocolate is an obsession with some people and irresistible to most of us. Its botanical name, *Theobrama cacao*, means "food for the gods", but ordinary mortals seem to become addicted to chocolate just as easily. Monthly magazines have even been devoted to it, printed with chocolate-scented ink. Perhaps word had spread that Madame de Pompadour recommended chocolate as an aphrodisiac and Casanova rated it above champagne for its seductive qualities.

Successful Cooking with Chocolate

The recipes in this book give clear, step-by-step instructions to help you achieve perfect results. However, there are some essential rules that should be followed carefully.

◆ Weigh out and prepare all ingredients before you start work on a recipe.

◆ Always use ingredients at room temperature; take eggs, butter and milk out of the refrigerator in good time (but not cream for whipping or it will separate).

◆ Follow the same units of measurement throughout; do not mix metric and imperial.

◆ All spoon measurements are level: 1 teaspoon = 5ml; 1 tablespoon = 15ml.

◆ All eggs are large unless otherwise stated.

◆ The correct-size baking tin is essential for cakes and pies. Measure across the top of the tin from one inside wall to the other. Disregard any other measurement marked on the tin.

◆ Switch on the oven before starting to make a recipe and ensure that it has reached the correct temperature before use.

◆ To ensure the oven temperature is correct, check with an oven thermometer put in the centre of the oven before putting in the dish to be baked.

◆ Baking times given in the recipes can only be a guide, because every oven varies. Check the dish 5 minutes before the end of the recommended cooking time, and leave in the oven or remove as necessary.

✳ **Warning: Raw or very lightly cooked eggs can transmit salmonella. Recipes with this warning should not be given to the elderly, young children and pregnant women.**

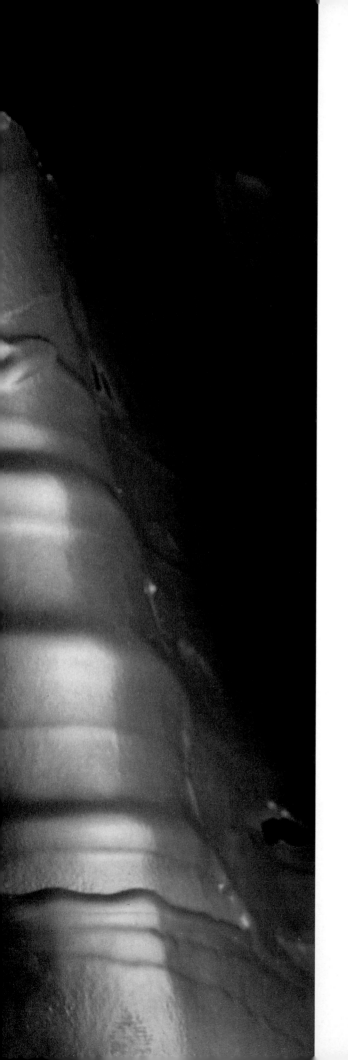

A Gallery of
Chocolate

These pages of gorgeous, taste bud-tingling chocolate cakes, desserts, confectionery, tarts, biscuits and rich sauces give a preview of *Ultimate Chocolate*'s wonderfully wide-ranging contents. They illustrate recipes, drawn from the cooking and baking traditions of many countries and cover all the ways in which chocolate may be used in cooking. Whichever dishes you choose to make, you are certain to give pleasure to everyone who loves chocolate.

Marbled Millefeuille
(See pages 106-7.)

Chocolate Layer Cakes

Above and opposite:
Pecan Chocolate Fudge
Cake (*See page 56.*)

Nothing tempts the chocolate-lover's taste-buds as thoroughly as a layer cake extravagantly filled with a chocolate buttercream crunchy with nuts, thickly whipped cream or a fruit-flavoured frosting. There is plenty of choice here, from classics like Black Forest Gâteau to everyone's favourite, Chocolate Layer Cake.

"On no other occasion has Nature concentrated in so small a space [the cocoa bean] such an abundance of the most valuable nourishment."

Alexander von Humboldt,
19th-century traveller

Gâteau Royale
(*See pages 58-9.*)

White Chocolate Cake
(*See page 61.*)

Below:
Black Forest Gâteau
(*See page 57.*)

Deliciously dark chocolate cake, sandwiched with rich creamy fillings and frostings

Dessert Cakes

Above and opposite:
Chocolate Truffle Cake
(See page 71.)

Stylishly decorated and richly flavoured dessert cakes and tortes have been a well-loved theme in continental pâtisserie for many generations. This irresistible selection brings together some of the most delectable chocolate dessert cakes, including the classic Austrian Sacher Torte, and a deliciously soft-textured Chocolate Truffle Cake.

"When I die," I said to my friend, "I'm not going to be embalmed. I'm going to be dipped." "Milk chocolate or bittersweet?" was her immediate concern.

Adrianne Marcus, *The Chocolate Bible* (1982)

Sacher Torte
(See page 72.)

Le Diabolo
(See page 75.)

See the glories of chocolate unfold in a myriad of decorative shapes and many melt-in-the-mouth textures. Delight in the luscious curls and lightly trailing swirls, the delicately veined leaves and finely drawn scrolls

Celestial Kumquat Torte
(See page 68.)

Chocolate Hazelnut Cake
(See page 70.)

Biscuits

Chocolate biscuits make the perfect snack, ideal with a glass of milk or cup of coffee, or just nibbled and relished on their own. Others are excellent accompaniments for desserts and ice creams. Most biscuit recipes are easy to make – although the decorating can be as elaborate as you like – and they store well, too.

Above and opposite:
Chocolate Hazelnut Tuiles
(See page 89.)

"I observe my chocolate diet, to which I believe I owe my health... It is admirable and delicious."

Marie de Villars,
wife of a French
ambassador, 1680

Crisp or chewy, round or heart-shaped, with fruit, nuts or peel: here are biscuits for everyone

Coconut
Macaroons
(See page 90.)

Florentines
(See page 84.)

Chocolate
Shortbreads
(See page 88.)

Mocha Biscuits
(See page 87.)

Pies & Tarts

Above and opposite:
Chocolate Banoffee Pie
(See page 99.)

Dessert pies and tarts with chocolate among the ingredients make impressive finales for any meal, with the added advantage of being easy to serve. Recipes include a French favourite, Chocolate Pear Tart, and American classics like Mississippi Mud Pie and a chocolate version of Pecan Pie.

"Chocolate is...a powerful restorative...Let men dose themselves with a good half-litre of amber-coloured chocolate... and they will see a miracle."

J. A. Brillat-Savarin,
Physiologie du goût (1825)

Savour the wonderful taste of chocolate mingling with pears, creamy toffee or crunchy nuts

Chocolate
Pear Tart
(See page 98.)

Chocolate
Chiffon Pie
(See page 95.)

Chocolate
Mousse Pie
(See page 94.)

Family favourites and classic recipes; chocolate whisked into light and delicate tarts

Cold Desserts

Above and opposite:
White Chocolate and Lime
Mousse *(See page 108.)*

Cold chocolate desserts and ices, however elaborate, can be prepared well in advance, making them ideal for dinner parties and special occasions. A beautifully presented layered chocolate terrine, scoops of chocolate mousse with a luscious sauce or a stunning iced soufflé will guarantee a successful finale to any meal.

"Chocolate is not only pleasant to taste, but it is a veritable balm of the mouth."

Dr S. Blancardi,
Amsterdam physician,
1705

Black and White Hazelnut Mousse
(See page 115.)

Chocolate Meringue
Sandwich
(See page 110.)

Marbled Millefeuille
(See page 107.)

Cool chocolate in mousses and soufflés; light-as-air chocolate layers in elegant terrines; ice-cold chocolate in frozen desserts and ice creams

White Chocolate
Ice Cream *(See page 120.)*

Confectionery

Above A basket of
Truffles and Candies

Fudge, responsible for awakening many a
childhood interest in cooking, is just one of a
variety of sweets that can be made at home.
Mints, chocolate-covered nuts, and Italian
panforte are within any cook's range. Chocolate
truffles are perhaps the easiest and most
delicious of all—and they look sumptuous, too.

*"The sweets I remember
best were...filled with
dark chocolate filling. If
I found one now I am
sure it would have the
same taste of hope."*

Graham Greene, writer

White chocolate-dipped
Truffle *(See page 124.)*

Armagnac Prune Truffle
(See page 122.)

Chocolate Truffle coated in
grated chocolate *(See page 124.)*

White Chocolate Truffle
(See page 125.)

Irresistibly stylish sweets and truffles filled with fruit, nuts and liqueur creams

Chocolate Truffle
(See page 124.)

Chocolate Truffle coated
in cocoa powder
(See page 124.)

White Chocolate Truffle with
chopped nut coating
(See page 125.)

ChocolateTruffle
(See page 124.)

Truffle with white
chocolate decoration
(See page 124.)

Chocolate Sauces

Above and opposite:
Bitter Chocolate Sauce
(See page 135.)

Sauces have an important role to play with sweet dishes. Whether it is a hot fudge sauce to be poured over ice cream, a warm chocolate sauce to serve with steamed pudding or a sharp raspberry coulis to contrast and mellow the richness of chocolate, sauces stimulate our visual appreciation as well as our palates.

"To a coffee-house, to drink jocolatte, very good"

Samuel Pepys,
Diary (1664)

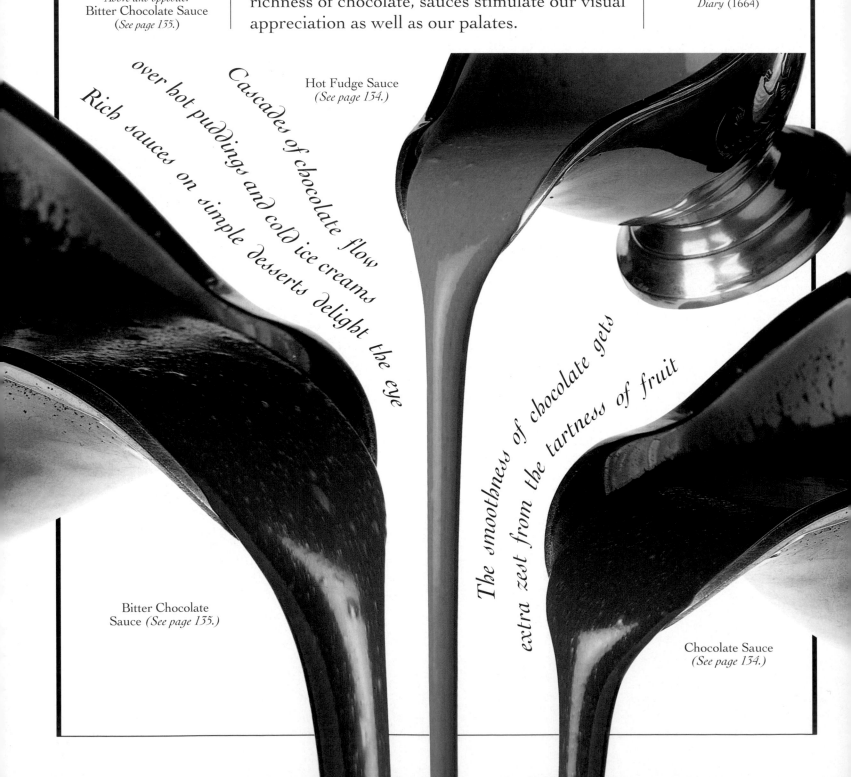

Hot Fudge Sauce
(See page 134.)

Cascades of chocolate flow over hot puddings and cold ice creams

Rich sauces on simple desserts delight the eye

The smoothness of chocolate gets extra zest from the tartness of fruit

Bitter Chocolate
Sauce *(See page 135.)*

Chocolate Sauce
(See page 134.)

The Essentials of
Cooking
with
Chocolate

Chocolate is an exciting ingredient to work with, especially when its unique properties are understood and the techniques of handling it have been mastered. This section deals with both. The different types of chocolate are described and illustrated, with detailed information on how each is best used in cooking. The basic techniques of chopping, melting and tempering chocolate are shown in clear step-by-step sequences. Also included are hints on buying and storing chocolate and on the essential kitchen tools and equipment needed for successful cooking with chocolate.

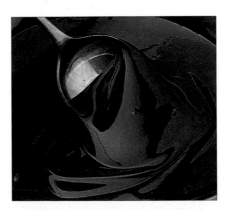

Melting chocolate
(See page 33.)

Making Chocolate

Chocolate, like coffee, originates in a bean, but one that grows on a tree, not a bush. The exotic cocoa tree produces a blizzard of pink and white flowers, green unripe fruit and bright golden cocoa pods, all at the same time. Encased in the pod is the dark little cocoa bean. Put through an intricate production process, the bean is transformed into cocoa mass, which ultimately becomes that magically pleasurable ingredient, chocolate.

THE COCOA TREE

The region between the 20th parallels, with the exception of parts of Africa, is the home of the cocoa tree. The tree begins to bear fruit once it is four years old and has an active lifespan of at least sixty years. Its fruit grows directly out of the older wood of the trunk and main branches, reaching the size of a small rugby football and ripening to a rich golden colour. Inside the ripe pods, purplish-brown cocoa beans are surrounded by pale pink pulp. After the pods are cut from the tree, beans and pulp are left to ferment together. The beans turn a dull red and develop their characteristic flavour. After fermentation, the beans are dried in the sun, acquiring their final "chocolate" colour. They are now ready for shipping to the manufacturing countries. Various bean types have been bred, and experts pride themselves on their ability to distinguish chocolate made from Criollo or Trinitario beans, say, from a Forastero.

PROCESSING THE BEANS

When the dried beans reach the processing plant, they are cleaned and checked for quality then roasted. Roasting, an important stage in the manufacturing process, develops the flavour of the beans and loosens the kernels from the hard outer shell. Each chocolate manufacturer has his own roasting secrets which contribute significantly to the chocolate's flavour. After roasting, the beans have a distinctive chocolatey smell. The next step is to crack the beans open, discarding their shells and husks, to obtain the kernels, called 'nibs'. It is the processing of these small, brown nibs that gives us chocolate. The roasted nibs, which contain on average 54 per cent cocoa butter, are ground into a dark, thick paste called cocoa "mass" or "solids". When more pressure is applied to the cocoa solids, the resulting products are cocoa butter and a solid cocoa cake. From the cocoa cake, crushed into cocoa crumb and then finely ground, comes cocoa powder.

Dried cocoa bean (above)

Cocoa pod (left)

Cocoa butter

Cocoa solids, or mass

Cocoa crumb

CONCHING

Chocolate is generally cocoa solids and sugar, with added cocoa butter, in the case of plain chocolate, or milk, in the case of milk chocolate, plus vanilla and other flavourings. Conching, in which the chocolate mixture is heated in huge vats and rotated with large paddles to blend it, is the final manufacturing process. Small additions of cocoa butter and lecithin, an emulsifier, are made to create the smooth, voluptuous qualities essential to the final product.

SWEETENING CHOCOLATE

Baking or bitter chocolate is simply cocoa solids and cocoa butter. To produce the great range of plain chocolates, from bittersweet to semisweet and sweet, more cocoa butter plus varying amounts of sugar, vanilla and lecithin are added. The flavour and sweetness of a plain chocolate will be unique to its maker, with one brand's bittersweet tasting like another brand's semisweet. Changing your usual brand of chocolate can make a difference to the flavour of a favourite recipe. To make milk chocolate, milk solids replace some of the cocoa solids. White chocolate is not, in fact, a real chocolate since it is made without cocoa solids; brands containing all cocoa butter, rather than vegetable oil, are best.

BUYING AND STORING CHOCOLATE

◆ Read the label. "Artificial chocolate" or "chocolate–flavoured" are not the real thing, as both flavour and texture will confirm.
◆ Note the percentages of cocoa solids and sugar on the label: these indicate the quality and taste of the chocolate.
◆ Store chocolate tightly wrapped in clingfilm, in a cool, dry, airy place, preferably at a constant temperature.
◆ Properly stored plain and bittersweet chocolate will keep for over a year.
◆ Milk and white chocolate should not be kept more than six months. Although the latter may taste fine, it does not melt well after long storage.
◆ Stored at warm temperatures chocolate will develop a "bloom" of surface streaks and blotches; at damp, cold temperatures a grey-white film may form. These changes will not greatly affect the flavour and texture of the chocolate and it can still be used for cooking and baking.

Types of Chocolate

A great range of excellent eating (dessert) and cooking chocolate is available in supermarkets as well as specialist shops. Differences between brands depend on the beans used, the proportion of cocoa solids and cocoa butter, and the sugar content and flavouring. The darkest plain chocolate contains the highest proportion of cocoa solids and cocoa butter, with chocolates called "continental" plain or dark containing up to 75 per cent cocoa solids. A good plain chocolate has a minimum 45–50 per cent cocoa solids. Less expensive brands substitute vegetable oils and shortening for the cocoa butter.

PLAIN CHOCOLATE

Plain chocolate is the type most commonly used as a baking ingredient.

COCOA POWDER

There are two types, the more mellow Dutch-processed or alkalized, and non-alkalized. The two are interchangeable in cooking. Drinking chocolate powder is not a substitute for cocoa.

CHOCOLATE CHIPS

Designed to keep their shape without melting during baking, these cannot replace cooking chocolate.

COUVERTURE

Also called dipping or coating chocolate, this fine-quality chef's chocolate is tempered before use as a coating chocolate (see page 35). Because of its high cocoa butter content, it melts smoothly and sets to a thin coating with a high glossy shine when it has been tempered. It is available in plain, white and milk chocolate varieties, in blocks and as chocolate drops.

Chocolate chips

Couverture

Plain chocolate, variously called bittersweet, semisweet, dark and continental dark or plain, is the main chocolate for cooking. All but bittersweet (available from specialist suppliers) contain enough sugar to make them sweet enough to eat.

Different brands contain varying amounts of cocoa solids and sugar. Check the packet label and use a brand that contains a minimum of 45–50% cocoa solids. "Continental" plain or dark chocolate contains as much as 75% cocoa solids.

MILK CHOCOLATE

Milk chocolate is often used as a decorative chocolate, making a perfect colour and taste contrast with plain chocolate.

In milk chocolate, milk solids (dried milk or condensed milk) replace some of the cocoa solids, giving it a sweet taste and smooth texture. The best brands are those that contain the highest percentage of cocoa solids and real vanilla.

Milk chocolate is not suitable for cooking. It is more sensitive to heat than plain chocolate, making it difficult to work with. It is very useful for decoration, however, making a good contrast to plain in both colour and flavour.

WHITE CHOCOLATE

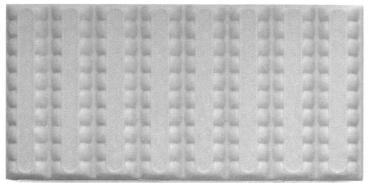

White chocolate has an extra sweet flavour that makes it popular for making confectionery.

White chocolate is technically not a real chocolate, since it does not contain cocoa solids. Better brands are made with a high proportion of cocoa butter as well as milk solids and sugar. Avoid those made with vegetable oil or fat.

As with milk chocolate, white chocolate does not tolerate heat and is usually melted but not baked. The added milk solids can cause it to turn grainy when heated too quickly. Its sweet but delicious flavour makes it popular with dessert chefs.

Basic Techniques

Chocolate is simple to work with, but needs careful handling. Knowing how to chop, grate, melt and temper chocolate correctly is the key to success because these techniques are basic to cooking and to making chocolate decorations. Master them and you will make deliciously simple desserts and adventurous chocolate creations with ease.

Chocolate is sensitive to atmosphere. Cool, dry air provides the best conditions for working with chocolate. If your kitchen is hot and steamy, chocolate will be difficult to handle. Avoid this problem by planning your chocolate baking or cooking session for a time when other cooking in the kitchen has been completed.

CHOPPING AND GRATING

Chocolate to be chopped or grated must be firm; chill it briefly before beginning. If you are grating or chopping by hand, handle the chocolate as little as possible, using a piece of paper to prevent it melting from the heat of your hands. Chop or grate on to a clean, dry surface, as moisture will affect the consistency of the chocolate if it is to be melted. To grate, use a large piece that is easy to handle, hold it firmly and work against the large grid of the grater.

Chop with a knife that has a large, sharp blade. Use the broad end, not the tip, and rock the edge of the blade over the chocolate until pieces break easily. Cut chocolate into even-sized pieces.

Fit a food processor with a metal blade. Put chocolate pieces into the machine, then use the pulse button to chop. Do not overwork, as the heat of the machine could melt the chocolate.

MELTING CHOCOLATE

Follow the method for melting chocolate described on page 33. Once the chocolate starts to melt, stir it occasionally until it is smooth, then remove it from the heat. Chocolates have different consistencies when melted: for example, bittersweet chocolate becomes runny, while plain and dark (continental plain) chocolates hold their shape until stirred. Thus, a chocolate may keep its shape when it is already soft and in danger of getting too hot. Keep heat low (no more than 44°C/110°F) to stop scorching and ruining the flavour.

Melting in a Microwave Oven
The inside of the microwave must be completely dry. Break the chocolate into even-sized pieces before putting it into a bowl for melting. Timing will depend on the output of the oven and the type and amount of chocolate being melted, but never melt chocolate on High. The chart on the right gives timings for a 650 watt oven; for ovens with a higher wattage, timings may be about 30 seconds less. Stirring the chocolate every 30 seconds during melting will enable you to keep a check on progress.

APPROXIMATE MELTING TIMES IN A 650 WATT MICROWAVE OVEN

Plain Chocolate

Quantity	On Medium
60g (2oz)	2 minutes
125g (4oz)	2½ minutes
180g (6oz)	3 minutes

Milk and White Chocolate

Quantity	On Low
60g (2oz)	2½ minutes
125g (4oz)	3 minutes
180g (6oz)	4 minutes

SUCCESSFUL MELTING

Chocolate should not be melted over direct heat. A double boiler or a water bath, made by putting a metal or glass bowl over a pan of water, are the best methods. The bottom of the bowl should not touch the water in the pan.

This chocolate is just starting to melt

1 Break or chop the chocolate into even-sized pieces and put in a metal or glass bowl. Smaller pieces will melt more quickly.

2 Put the bowl over a pan of hot, but not simmering (bubbling), water. Once the chocolate starts to melt, stir it occasionally to push unmelted pieces into the melted chocolate.

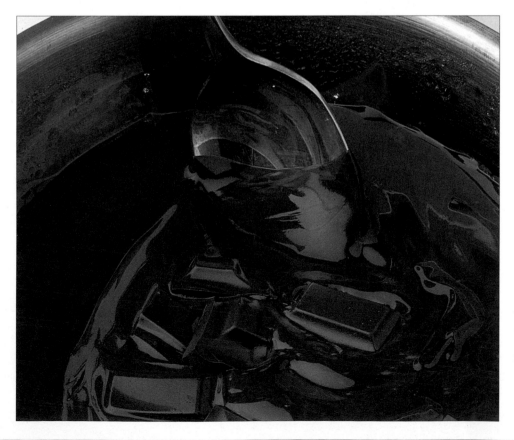

3 When completely melted, chocolate should have a smooth, glossy texture. Chocolate that has been allowed to overheat will separate or "seize", turning into a rough mass. Rescue seized chocolate by stirring in 1 teaspoon warm vegetable oil, repeating if necessary.

PREPARING MELTED CHOCOLATE FOR CURLS AND CUT-OUTS

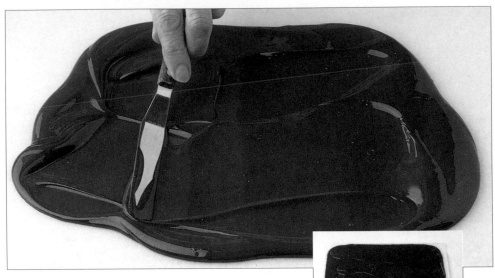

1 For decorations such as curls, caraque and cut-outs, pour melted chocolate on to a clean, smooth work surface such as an acrylic board.

2 Using a palette knife, spread the chocolate across the surface with even strokes. The chocolate should be of a uniform thickness so it sets evenly.

Spread chocolate to about 1.5mm (1/16 in) thick

MELTING CHOCOLATE WITH OTHER INGREDIENTS

Butter or oil can be melted with chocolate or added during melting without putting it at risk. Chocolate can be melted with a liquid as long as there is enough of it – at least 1 tablespoon of liquid per 60g (2oz) of chocolate.

Ingredients for melting with chocolate must be at a similar temperature. Adding a hotter liquid can cause the chocolate to seize. Adding a cold ingredient straight from the refrigerator can make the chocolate lumpy.

1 Ensure that the butter has been removed from the refrigerator ahead of time so that is at room temperature before using. Melt the chocolate, then remove it from the heat.

2 Gently stir the butter into the melted chocolate with a rubber spatula to ensure a smooth texture.

COMBINING MELTED CHOCOLATE WITH OTHER INGREDIENTS

Many recipes include a step where chocolate is melted, or combined in its melted form, with other ingredients. Here are some simple tips to follow:

◆ Let melted chocolate cool to room temperature before adding it to cake mixtures and biscuit doughs. If the chocolate is too hot, it can melt the fat in the mixture and cause a change in the texture of the final baked product.

◆ Melted chocolate added to a light mixture, like creamed sugar and butter, should be whisked in quickly in a warm place to keep the chocolate fluid.

◆ Use a wooden spoon to mix melted chocolate into a thick mixture like egg yolks and sugar. Steady the bowl while beating in the chocolate.

◆ In a microwave, chocolate takes less time to melt with butter or liquid than when melted on its own.

◆ White chocolate has a tendency to seize easily. It should be treated with extra care when being melted or combined with any ingredient.

TEMPERING COUVERTURE

The tempering process prevents couverture from looking dull and streaky once it has been melted and then solidifies. Melted couverture is mixed with other ingredients in recipes. When couverture is used on its own for coating and decorations, the tempering gives it a crisp, glossy finish which remains shiny for weeks without refrigeration. The chocolate also shrinks slightly, allowing it to be released easily from a mould.

1 Melt the chopped chocolate (see page 33). Stir the melting chocolate gently until the temperature reaches 45°C (113°F) on a chocolate thermometer and the consistency is very smooth.

Spread evenly with a small palette knife

3 Work the chocolate using a plastic scraper or spatula, spreading it back and forth across the board and then back over itself.

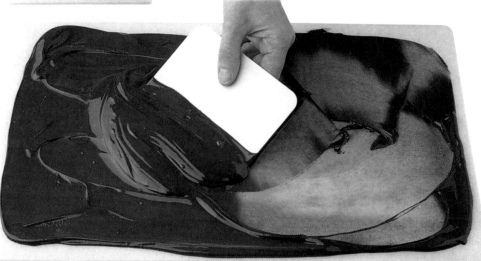

2 Pour three-quarters of the chocolate on to a cool, smooth work surface, such as an acrylic board or a marble slab. Spread evenly with a palette knife. The surface must be clean and dry.

4 After a few minutes, the chocolate will have thickened as it cooled. The chocolate is ready when its temperature is 28°C (82°F). Using the scraper, return the chocolate to the remaining chocolate in the bowl.

5 Sit the bowl over a saucepan of hot water and stir the chocolates gently together with a rubber spatula until they are well blended.

6 Stir the chocolate constantly over the hot water until its temperature has returned to 32°C (90°F); the chocolate should be smooth and glossy.

7 The tempered chocolate should be used at once. Keep it over warm water to retain the correct temperature. It can be tempered again, if necessary.

Essential Tools

Here is a selection of useful equipment for cooking with chocolate. Several items, found in most kitchens, are included here because they are essential to specifically chocolate-related techniques.

When buying tools, always choose the best quality available: they last longer, are more reliable and achieve the best results. Once you are familiar with the techniques in the book, your own essentials will be added to this list.

Acrylic board

Vegetable peeler makes curls easily

Large kitchen knife

Stainless steel box grater

Wooden spoon

Metal spoon

Long-handled rubber-bladed spatula

Sugar thermometer

Chocolate thermometer

A knife for chopping chocolate should have a long broad blade with a sharp edge. A clean acrylic board has many uses. Use it to spread out chocolate when making decorations and tempering. A marble surface sometimes allows chocolate to cool and harden too quickly.

A vegetable peeler and grater are everyday kitchen tools that are also useful for chocolate. The large grid of the grater makes small chocolate curls and grates chocolate. The vegetable peeler also makes chocolate curls.

Mixing and stirring heated ingredients is best done with a long-handled wooden spoon. Use metal spoons for folding in flour and whisked egg whites. Flexible rubber spatulas scrape every bit from the sides of a bowl.

A saucepan and a heatproof bowl that fits firmly into it make a perfect water bath for melting chocolate. Choose a glass bowl that allows you to monitor the hot water in the pan: it must not bubble.

Bowls made out of strong heatproof glass with smooth, rounded bottoms are best for melting chocolate in a microwave or water bath.

Thermometers should be well tested before using. The small red-topped thermometer is a chocolate thermometer. The large sugar thermometer is an essential tool when boiling sugar syrups for buttercreams and some cakes.

Essential Tools

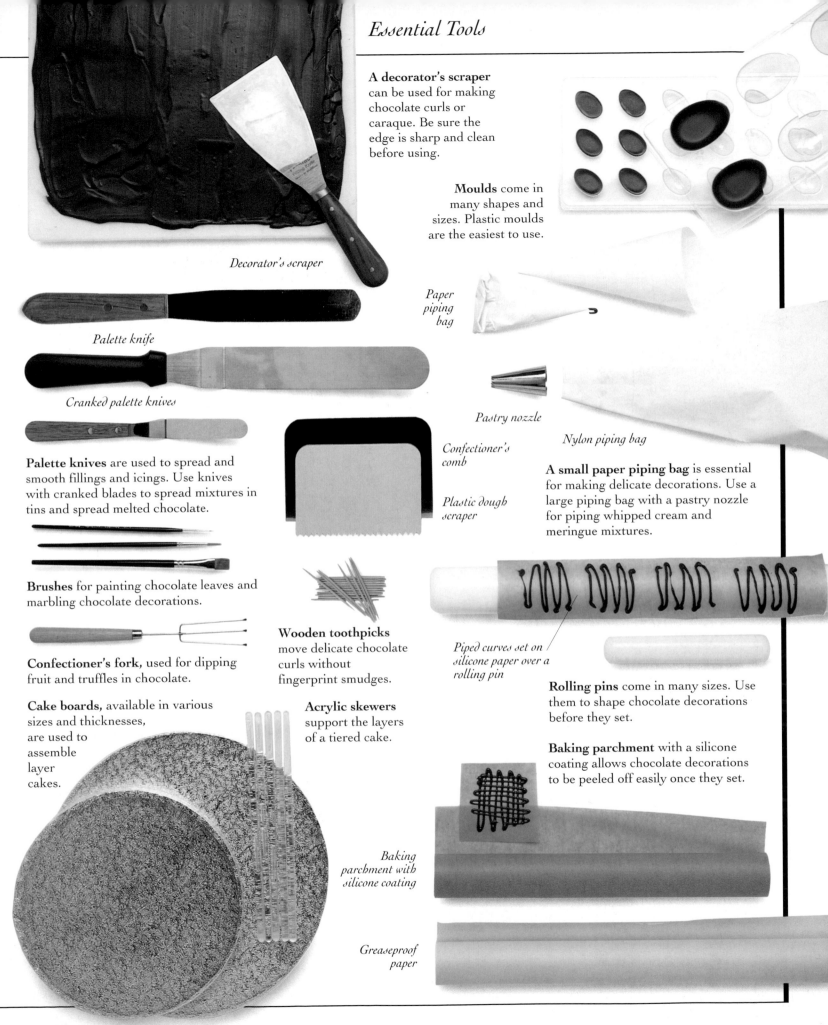

A decorator's scraper can be used for making chocolate curls or caraque. Be sure the edge is sharp and clean before using.

Moulds come in many shapes and sizes. Plastic moulds are the easiest to use.

Decorator's scraper

Palette knife

Cranked palette knives

Palette knives are used to spread and smooth fillings and icings. Use knives with cranked blades to spread mixtures in tins and spread melted chocolate.

Brushes for painting chocolate leaves and marbling chocolate decorations.

Confectioner's fork, used for dipping fruit and truffles in chocolate.

Cake boards, available in various sizes and thicknesses, are used to assemble layer cakes.

Paper piping bag

Pastry nozzle

Nylon piping bag

Confectioner's comb

Plastic dough scraper

A small paper piping bag is essential for making delicate decorations. Use a large piping bag with a pastry nozzle for piping whipped cream and meringue mixtures.

Piped curves set on silicone paper over a rolling pin

Wooden toothpicks move delicate chocolate curls without fingerprint smudges.

Acrylic skewers support the layers of a tiered cake.

Rolling pins come in many sizes. Use them to shape chocolate decorations before they set.

Baking parchment with a silicone coating allows chocolate decorations to be peeled off easily once they set.

Baking parchment with silicone coating

Greaseproof paper

Working with Chocolate

DO'S & DON'TS OF MELTING CHOCOLATE

◆ Do cut chocolate into even-sized pieces to melt.

◆ Don't melt chocolate over direct heat.

◆ Do use a water bath with a glass bowl so you can check that the water does not bubble too strongly.

◆ Don't allow the hot water to touch the bowl.

◆ Do melt chocolate slowly to achieve the smoothest results.

◆ Don't cover the bowl of chocolate while it is melting; condensation forming under the cover could drop into the chocolate and damage it.

◆ Do wipe the inside of the microwave completely dry before using it to melt chocolate.

◆ Do watch milk and white chocolates carefully, they will burn and seize more easily than plain.

◆ Do melt chocolate with a good quantity of liquid – at least 1 tbsp per 60g/2oz chocolate.

◆ Don't forget to have all the ingredients at room temperature before starting a recipe.

What do I do when chocolate turns lumpy?

◆ Chocolate that has gone lumpy or grainy can be rescued by stirring in one or two teaspoons of vegetable oil until smooth.

Is there any way to save chocolate once it has been 'scorched' or burned?

◆ When chocolate is heated over direct heat, or a water bath gets too hot too quickly, chocolate will burn. Once the flavour of the chocolate has been affected, it cannot be saved.

What if I've carefully melted chocolate with a safe amount of liquid and I know it hasn't burned, but it seizes anyway?

◆ Chocolate that has gone grainy and hard can sometimes be rescued by adding extra liquid to loosen it. The water or other liquid should be the same temperature as the seized chocolate and should be added one tablespoon at a time. Add each tablespoon all at once and whisk vigorously. Repeat if necessary.

PREPARING CHOCOLATE FOR DECORATIONS

When do I need to temper my chocolate? What happens if I don't?

◆ It is not necessary to temper chocolate, whether plain or couverture, when it is used in everyday cooking. Tempered couverture is essential to achieve a professional, glossy finish on confectionery and chocolate decorations. This finish also allows confectionery to be kept at room temperature without losing its glossy lustre.

◆ Couverture that is untempered will "bloom", becoming dull and streaky, when it dries.

How can I use untempered couverture for decorating or covering confectionery?

◆ Mixing couverture with equal quantities of chocolate-flavour cake covering gives an easily worked chocolate, though the finish is less crisp.

When making chocolate curls, what should I do if the chocolate splinters instead of curling?

◆ This means the chocolate is too hard. Wave a hand-held hairdryer, on the lowest temperature, over the chocolate for a few seconds. Try again.

When making chocolate curls, what should I do if the chocolate melts and sticks to the scraper?

◆ This means the chocolate is too soft. Put the board of chocolate into the refrigerator for 30–60 seconds to harden a little. Try again.

When should I refrigerate a finished chocolate recipe and when should I avoid the refrigerator?

◆ Put decorations and dipped confections made with untempered chocolate in the refrigerator immediately they are made. This will "freeze" the fat crystals and prevent spoiling the glossy finish.

◆ Tortes and cakes that have been glazed and stored at room temperature after making will be spoiled if they are later put in the refrigerator. Chilling makes them dense and hard and dulls the finish of the glaze.

PREPARING CAKE TINS

The correct type and size tin is crucial to successful cake baking. Preparing a cake tin helps to stop the cake from sticking, making it easier to remove. Odd-shaped tins should be greased twice with butter, then dusted with flour. Other tins can be lined with silicone paper, which has a non-stick finish, or greaseproof paper, which needs to be brushed with more butter.

HELPFUL TIPS

◆ *All bakeware should be clean and dry before you start.*

◆ *Greasing before lining keeps the paper in place.*

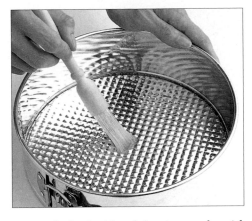

1 Brush the inside of the tin evenly with melted butter. Cut one strip of paper to fit around the sides, overlapping slightly, making sure it is 5cm (2in) wider than the depth of the tin.

2 Fold in one long edge of the paper by 2.5cm (1in) and crease well. Unfold and then make angled cuts at 2.5cm (1in) intervals along this edge, up to the folded line.

3 Drop the paper strip cut-side down into the tin so that the creased edge rests in the join at the base of the tin. Press the paper well on to the buttered sides and base of the cake tin.

4 Place the base of the tin on another piece of paper. Draw a faint pencil line around the base. Cut out the circle just inside the pencil line so the paper disc fits snugly into the bottom.

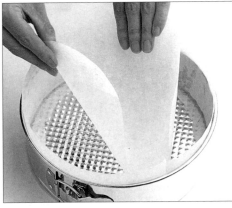

5 Smooth the paper circle on the base of the tin, making sure that the cut edge lies flat underneath it. If using greaseproof paper, brush once more with melted butter.

TOAST AND SKIN HAZELNUTS

Hazelnuts seem to have a special affinity with chocolate, and the two are combined in several recipes in this book. Toasting hazelnuts allows their papery skins to be removed easily.

1 Preheat the oven to 180°C/ 350°F/gas 4. Spread the nuts on a baking sheet. Bake for 8 minutes.

2 Tip the hot nuts on to a cloth. Fold the cloth over them and rub gently to remove the skins. Cool before using.

Decorating
with
Chocolate

It is the decorative touches – curls, fans, ribbons, flowers and leaves, curves, waves and cut-outs – that personalize chocolate cakes, desserts, small cakes and biscuits, making them uniquely special. This section explains how to make many kinds of decoration with a professional finish, from easily made simple effects with melted chocolate to more elaborate decorations based on piping chocolate, including feathering, marbling and other patterns. Making and using fillings and coverings, which are essential bases for many decorations, complete the section in impressive style.

Marbled Chocolate Eggs
(See page 129.)

Making Decorations

Chocolate decorations enhance the appearance of desserts and cakes and offer opportunities for creating original displays of chocolate perfection. The decorations here, all of them used in recipes in this book, cover a wide range, from easy to intricate.

Elaborate decorations, such as piped shapes and marbled curls, require practice to master. Others, like cut-out shapes and leaves, are easier for the beginner to tackle. Take a free afternoon to practise making decorations. Always start with chocolate that is firm and at room temperature, since cold chocolate cracks easily and too soft chocolate can become sticky. Trial runs will not waste expensive chocolate, since failed efforts can go back into the melting bowl, and any items successfully completed can be kept for several days, or even weeks, until the opportunity arises to use them. Most decorations can be stored in an airtight container in the refrigerator. They may also be frozen, separated between sheets of greaseproof paper. Wrap larger pieces, such as baskets, waves and large curls, in clingfilm before putting them in containers. Milk and white chocolate decorations will keep for two weeks in the refrigerator; couverture and plain chocolate ones will keep for four weeks.

GRATED

Grated chocolate, an easily made decoration

1 Use a large piece of chocolate that is easy to handle. Chill the chocolate in the refrigerator briefly to firm it before grating. If your hands are very warm, hold the chocolate in a piece of paper to prevent melting.

2 Work the chocolate against the large grid of the grater, as in the picture above. Grate the chocolate on to a plate or greaseproof paper.

Note: As an alternative, a food processor fitted with a grater disc can also be used. Break chocolate into chunky pieces. Feed the pieces of chocolate through the feeder tube while the machine is running.

QUICK CURLS

For wide curls use the flat underside of the peeler

Store between sheets of grease-proof paper in the refrigerator

Curls are quickly made with a vegetable peeler

1 Use a large, thick bar of chocolate at room temperature. Scrape the chocolate firmly along its length with a sharp, swivel-type vegetable peeler. For narrow curls, use one of the edges; for fat curls use the flat underside of the peeler.

2 If curls splinter or crack, the chocolate is too cold. Rub the chocolate with your thumb to soften it a little. If the chocolate becomes too soft, put it in the refrigerator briefly.

Note: Pressure applied on the block of chocolate will also affect the size of the curls. Applying firm pressure will result in larger, sturdier curls.

CARAQUE

Using a large-bladed knife to make caraque

1 Spread chocolate on an acrylic board (see page 34). Let it set firmly. Have a large-bladed knife ready.

2 Brace the board against your body. Starting about 5cm (2in) from the left corner of the board furthest from you, pull the knife blade towards you at a 45° angle, scraping along the chocolate to form a caraque, as above.

3 Use the knife blade to lift each piece of caraque off the board as you make it.

Note: For striped caraque, spread stripes of different coloured chocolates, touching, on the board.

CURLS

Chocolate fans /

Making curls with a decorator's scraper

1 Begin with a work surface spread with a thin layer of chocolate (see page 34). Allow the chocolate to set firmly at room temperature before starting. Have ready a decorator's scraper that is thoroughly clean.

2 Start 2.5cm (1in) from the nearest edge of chocolate. Push the decorator's scraper away from you at about a 25° angle across the surface of the chocolate until a large curl forms, as shown above. Use the scraper to lift the curl off the board as it is made.

3 To form chocolate fans, push the scraper forward, then pull it at a sharp angle, about 10°, to one side.

LEAVES

Real leaves are used to make this decoration

1 Use pliable leaves with well-defined veins, such as rose leaves. Artichoke leaves are excellent for making large roses. Be sure leaves are chemical-free, cleaned and dry.

2 Hold the leaf by its stem and use a small paint brush or pastry brush to coat a smooth layer of melted chocolate on the underside of the leaf, as shown above. Be careful not to drip chocolate over the edge of the leaf or it will be difficult to peel off.

3 Place, coated side up, on a baking sheet lined with silicone paper, and refrigerate until set. Peel leaf away from the chocolate; see the insert.

RIBBONS

Piped lines of white chocolate decorate these ribbons, used on the Wedding Cake (see pages 66–7)

Set the ends of longer ribbons into an egg box to turn them upwards.

Ribbons become curved when set over a rolling pin

1 Cut non-stick baking parchment into strips the width and length of the ribbons you plan to use.

2 Allow 125g (4oz) melted chocolate for about a dozen ribbons 1.5cm (¾in) wide and 15cm (6in) long.

3 Holding each end of a paper strip, dip just one side of the strip into the melted chocolate to coat it.

4 Lay the coated strip over a rolling pin to form a curve, as shown above. If liked, also put the ends of long ribbons into egg box compartments to turn them upwards. Allow to set, then peel off the paper.

WAVES

Melted chocolate sets into waves over chopsticks

1 Cut plastic bubble wrap or baking parchment into pieces the width of the waves you are planning to make.

2 Melt 60g (2oz) chocolate for a wave approx. 23 x 30cm (9 x 12in). Lay three chopsticks slightly apart on a work surface. Secure each one in place with tape, as above.

3 Spread the bubble wrap or paper with a thick layer of melted chocolate. Arrange over the sticks, as shown in the picture above; secure one end to the board with tape.

4 Allow to harden; carefully peel off the paper just before using.

BASKETS

Use a small, cranked palette knife to spread chocolate evenly

Chocolate baskets set into pretty folds

1 Cut plastic bubble wrap or baking parchment into four pieces, each 12cm (5in) square.

2 Melt 125g (4oz) chocolate to make four baskets. Spread the squares of bubble wrap or baking parchment with a thin layer of chocolate, leaving a narrow border.

3 Holding the squares by their clean corners, set each one gently into a small, shallow bowl or wide-mouthed glass or goblet, as shown above.

4 Put the bowls in the refrigerator until ready to use. Carefully peel the wrap away from the chocolate.

CUT-OUTS

Gently peel back the parchment paper from the chocolate

A sharp knife easily cuts the chocolate into shapes

1 Melt plain chocolate. Cut two pieces of baking parchment large enough to cover your work board.

2 Put one piece of parchment on the board and spread it with melted chocolate in an even layer about 1.5mm (1/16in) thick.

3 Allow to cool at room temperature. Once the chocolate is firm, flip the work board and the chocolate-coated parchment paper over on to the second piece of parchment.

4 Peel the paper away from the chocolate. Cut into desired shapes with a sharp knife, as shown above.

BOXES

For the box, cut two 10cm (4in) squares for the base and lid; cut four sides 10 x 2.5cm (4 x 1in) (cut 2 sides a little wider for overlap)

Melted chocolate holds the box's pieces together

1 This marbled chocolate box (shown with truffles on page 123) requires 150g (5oz) plain chocolate and 60g (2oz) white chocolate.

2 Melt the plain chocolate and spread it in a thin layer on an 18 x 23cm (7 x 9in) piece of baking parchment. To create the marbling with the white chocolate, see page 47.

3 Trim the chocolate and cut it into rectangles (see above for sizes). Melt chocolate trimmings. Use this chocolate to brush along the outside edges of the base rectangle, as shown above. Attach the sides to the base by cementing with the melted chocolate.

COMBING

Use prongs of a fork to make wavy lines

This melted chocolate decoration includes piping (see page 46)

A fork quickly combs a pattern into chocolate

1 Use a confectioner's comb or a fork, to make an attractive decoration on biscuits like Florentines (see recipe on page 84).

2 Melt plain, milk or white chocolate or, for a stunning effect, tempered couverture.

3 Hold the biscuit between thumb and forefinger and dip its base gently into the melted chocolate.

4 Put it on a wire rack, chocolate side up. When the chocolate is slightly set, gently drag the comb or fork across the chocolate, using a wavy motion, as shown above.

MAKING A PIPING BAG

Melted chocolate and thin icings are easily piped with a homemade paper piping bag. Cut a very small opening in the tip of the bag so that you can control the flow of the chocolate.

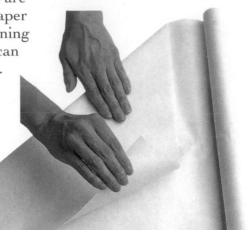

1 Unroll a length of greaseproof paper. Fold one corner of the paper across to meet the opposite corner of an imaginary square. Crease the fold and cut along it to remove a triangle of paper.

2 Fold the triangle in half. Place on a flat surface, with its long side facing you. Bring the right-hand point up and across to meet the middle point.

3 Now, fold the paper twice to the left to meet the left point. Squeeze the cone to open. Fold down the top edge of the cone above the seam to secure.

4 Open the cone and gently spoon the icing into the finished bag. For best results, fill the bag just half-way.

5 Fold over the top to seal, turning in the corners. Snip off the tip when ready to use. Hold the cone upright to prevent the icing from running out.

PIPING CHOCOLATE

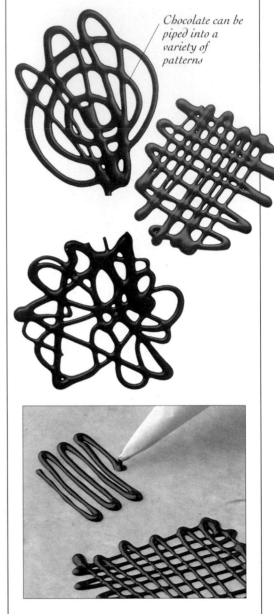

Chocolate can be piped into a variety of patterns

Piping patterns on to baking parchment

1 Sketch a series of simple patterns on to baking parchment. Turn the paper over and put on a baking sheet.

2 Spoon cooled, melted chocolate into a paper piping bag so it is no more than half full. Seal the bag and snip off a small piece of the tip.

3 Pipe the chocolate evenly on to the paper, using the lines of your patterns as a guide, as shown above.

4 Allow the chocolate to set, then remove the outlines from the paper by gently lifting them off with a palette knife.

CHOCOLATE CURVES

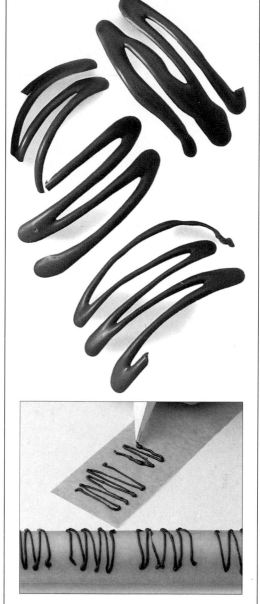

Piped curves are set over a rolling pin

1 Melt some plain chocolate and cool it so it just coats the back of a spoon. Half fill a paper piping bag, then seal it and snip the tip.

2 Pipe lines backwards and forwards across a strip of silicone-coated baking parchment, as shown above.

3 Carefully lift the strip of baking parchment and place over a rolling pin, as shown. Secure the strip in place with sticky tape.

4 Allow chocolate to set. Remove the curves by first lifting strip off the rolling pin and then gently peeling paper away from the chocolate curves.

FEATHERING

Feathering lines of chocolate with a toothpick

1 Melt some white chocolate and cool until it just coats the back of a spoon. Half fill a paper piping bag with the chocolate, seal, and snip tip.

2 Glaze the top of a cake or a batch of biscuits with melted plain chocolate.

3 While the chocolate glaze is still wet, pipe evenly spaced parallel lines of melted white chocolate over the plain chocolate.

4 Draw the tip of a toothpick through the white chocolate, first in one direction and then in the other, as shown above.

MARBLING

Marbling is incorporated into this chocolate wave (see page 44)

Marbling must be done on wet chocolate

1 Melt some white chocolate and cool until it just coats the back of a spoon. Half fill a paper piping bag with the chocolate, seal, and snip tip.

2 Melt some plain chocolate. Cut a piece of baking parchment and spread with the chocolate, leaving a narrow border clean.

3 While the plain chocolate is still wet, pipe a fine line of white chocolate in a looped scribble across the full width of the chocolate.

4 Draw the tip of a toothpick through the white chocolate lines to make swirls, as shown above.

MOULDED FLOWERS

This rose has chocolate marzipan leaves (see page 76)

Fitting rose petals round the central cone

1 Use either shop-bought chocolate modelling paste or chocolate marzipan (see page 76). Roll a small piece into a cone shape about 2.5cm (1in) long for the centre of the rose.

2 Pinch off pea-sized pieces of paste or marzipan and flatten between thumb and forefinger into petals, gently turning back the tips. Make some petals larger than others.

3 Fit one petal round the cone, as in the picture above, then add others so that each new petal partially covers the one before it; as in the completed roses at top. Finish the rose with large petals around the outside.

FILLING A PIPING BAG

A nylon piping bag fitted with a nozzle is best for piping whipped cream and thick buttercreams. A medium star nozzle is a good all-purpose size to choose.

To pipe rosettes, hold the bag upright and pipe in a circular motion to form a peaked swirl

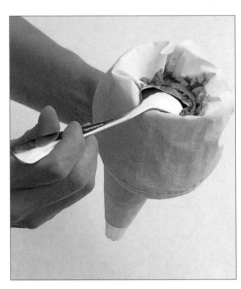

1 Drop the nozzle into the bag, pushing it firmly into the end. Hold the bag half-way up and fold back excess fabric over your hand.

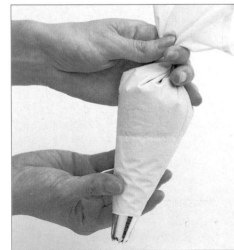

2 Half fill the bag, pushing the icing or cream down to remove air pockets. Unfold the fabric and twist it tightly just above the filling.

Rope design   Shell design

Squeeze the bag gently from the top when piping cream or icing

3 Squeeze the top of the bag with a firm and even pressure. Re-twist the bag as it empties to keep the filling together at all times.

Fillings and Toppings

A smooth covering of icing can turn a simple cake into an elegant conclusion to the perfect meal or into an appealing centrepiece for afternoon tea. Add lustre to a cake by using a simple glaze: the glossy coating can become the blank canvas for additional decorations. Use the techniques explained here to create flawless finishes and scrumptious fillings.

HOW TO MAKE A GLAZE

Adding a glaze, such as the Chocolate Glaze on page 136, to a cake gives it an elegant and glossy mirror-like finish. The glaze can be poured directly on to the cake, as with the Celestial Kumquat Torte on page 68. For an even smoother, finer finish, ice the cake with a preliminary coat of cooled, partially set glaze, then glaze it again with the rewarmed mixture, as with the Chocolate Hazelnut Cake on page 70.

1 Break chocolate into pieces and put with the butter and golden syrup in the top of a double boiler or over a water bath until melted.

2 Set aside and allow it to cool to a spreadable consistency (it should coat the back of a spoon). Use the glaze according to the recipe being followed.

GLAZING A CAKE TWICE

Giving a cake a preliminary coat of glaze holds crumbs in place and creates an even base for the final glossy coating.

1 Cool the glaze to a spreadable consistency (it should coat the back of a spoon). Use a palette knife to spread about a quarter of the glaze over the top and sides of the cake.

2 Allow the glaze to set firmly; reheat the remaining glaze and pour it over the top of the cake for the final finish.

Reheat the glaze to a pourable consistency to cover

Put cake on a wire rack set over a plate to catch the drips from the glaze. Excess glaze can be rewarmed and used again

CHOCOLATE GANACHE

This classic chocolate cream, for which the standard recipe is given on page 136, is used as a deliciously rich filling and as a covering for layer cakes, roulades, choux pastry and meringues. The recipe on page 136 can also be used as a sauce. The cream and chocolate should be whisked together only until they are blended. The method for making ganache described here is not suitable for using when making ganache as a sauce.

1 Melt the chocolate (see page 33) and set aside to cool. Whip the double cream until it forms soft peaks. Fold a large spoonful of cream into the cooled chocolate.

2 Fold the chocolate mixture into the remaining whipped cream. The ganache is best used soon after it is made. Makes enough to fill and cover one double layer cake.

CHOCOLATE FROSTING

There are many recipes for chocolate frosting. The methods may differ, but the basic recipe is much the same. This book's basic recipe uses equal amounts of chocolate and cream, plus butter for a silky result, as with the Pecan Chocolate Fudge Cake on page 56, or milk for a lighter texture, as with the Chocolate Almond and Raspberry Roulade on page 63. The basic proportions used here are 350g (12½oz) chocolate and 350ml (12fl oz) double cream, and 45g (1½oz) butter.

1 Break the chocolate into even-sized pieces and put it into a bowl. Bring the cream to the boil and pour over the chocolate. Stir gently to blend.

2 Cut the butter into small cubes and stir it into the mixture. Beat the mixture with a wooden spoon or wire whisk until thick enough to spread.

CUTTING CAKE IN LAYERS

Place the cake on a firm, level surface. Rest one hand lightly on top of the cake to hold it steady. Slice the cake horizontally through the centre with a sharp, long-bladed, serrated knife. When there are several layers, start with the top layer. Carefully separate the layers by sliding a thin cake board between them. Lift off and set aside.

FILLING AND ICING A CAKE

1 Begin with the bottom layer. Spread it evenly with a portion of the filling, to within 5mm (¼in) of the edge. Put a second cake layer on top, pressing it down gently.

2 Use a palette knife to spread the icing in an even layer over the top of the cake, using a paddling action so that the icing runs smoothly down the sides of the cake.

3 Use a generous amount of icing and make light, even strokes with the palette knife in order to cover the sides cleanly without spreading crumbs into the finished icing.

FINISHING THE SIDES OF A CAKE

While the glaze is still sticky, decorate the sides of an iced cake with grated chocolate, chopped nuts or praline, balance the cake on the palm of one hand. Hold it over a plate of coating. Lift coating on to sides of the cake with a large palette knife, pressing gently so the coating stays in place.

MAKING ALMOND PRALINE

1 Measure out 100g (3½oz) granulated sugar and 100g (3½oz) shelled unblanched almonds.

2 Oil a marble surface or baking sheet. Put the nuts and sugar in a small heavy-based saucepan. Set the pan over a low heat until the sugar starts to melt.

3 Continue cooking, stirring occasionally with a wooden spoon, until the sugar caramelizes and is a deep golden colour. The nuts should make a popping sound as they toast.

4 Pour the praline quickly on to the prepared surface. Spread out and leave until cold and hard.

5 Break into pieces and grind to the required consistency in a food processor or blender.

6 The praline will keep for several weeks in an air-tight container at room temperature.

A COMBED FINISH

After a cake has been covered with a smooth icing, the sides can be marked into horizontal lines with a confectioner's comb. Hold the comb vertically and drag it quickly but firmly through the set covering. The technique is not suitable for glossy icings.

Recipes

Here are more than one hundred delectable recipes, all demonstrating the unique qualities of chocolate, as a food and as an ingredient in cooking. There are recipes for everything from cakes and biscuits to hand-made chocolates and spectacular desserts, and recipes specially devised for important occasions like birthdays and weddings, or annual celebrations like Easter, Christmas and Valentine's Day. There are many American and European favourites as well as more recently created recipes.

Gâteau Royale
(See pages 58–9)

Rich Layer Cakes

Layer cakes, richly filled and sumptuously decorated, tempt the eye as well as the taste buds. Layered cakes here range from the light sponge of the airy-textured Gâteau Royale to the intensely dark Pecan Chocolate Fudge Cake. In other cakes, the layers are not so obvious: two roulades turn single layers of cake into wheels within wheels and a pound cake twists chocolate and vanilla layers into each other for a marbled effect. Ending this section is the ultimate layer cake: a beribboned, three-tiered Wedding Cake.

Chocolate Layer Cake

A very quick and easy cake to make and one of my family's favourites. The cake, which has the texture of a firm brownie, is sliced into thin layers, sandwiched together with whipped cream.

INGREDIENTS

For the cake

125g (4oz) unsalted butter
60g (2oz) cocoa powder, sifted
2 eggs
250g (8oz) caster sugar
1 tsp vanilla extract
60g (2oz) plain flour
60g (2oz) self-raising flour

For the filling and decoration

2 tbsp milk
450ml (¾pint) double cream
2 tbsp caster sugar
½ tsp vanilla extract
plain chocolate curls (see page 43)

1 Gently melt the butter in a saucepan, then stir in the cocoa until blended. Set aside. Beat the eggs with the sugar and vanilla until light, then stir in the cocoa mixture.

2 Sift the flours together twice. Sift them over the egg mixture, a third at a time, folding each one in with a metal spoon. Turn into the prepared tin and bake in the preheated oven for 40–45 minutes, or until a skewer inserted in the centre comes out clean.

3 Run a knife around the inside edge of the tin and leave the cake for 10 minutes before turning out on to a wire rack to cool completely. When the cake is cold, wrap it in foil and chill overnight. Although this is not absolutely necessary, it makes the cake easier to slice.

4 With the cake at room temperature, cut it into 4 equal layers, using a long serrated knife (see page 50). The cake layers will be very thin, so use two palette knives to move them.

5 For the filling, add the milk to the cream and whip until it forms soft peaks. Fold in the sugar and vanilla.

6 Use the top layer, cut side up, as the base. Cover it with some of the cream. Add a second layer and cover with cream; repeat with a third layer. Finish with the bottom layer, cut side down. Cover the top and sides of the cake with the remaining cream and decorate with chocolate curls.

VARIATION
Chocolate Praline Layer Cake
Use 1 quantity praline (see page 51). Fold 8 tablespoons of praline into two-thirds of the whipped cream. Use the plain whipped cream for one layer and the praline cream for two. Cover the top and sides of the cake with the rest of the praline cream. Use the remaining praline to coat the sides of the cake (see page 51). Decorate the top with chocolate curls.

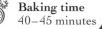

Oven temperature
180°C/350°F/gas 4

Baking time
40–45 minutes

Baking tin
20cm (8in) cake tin, greased and base-lined

Makes
8–10 slices

Storage
Unfilled cake keeps for 4–5 days, wrapped, in the refrigerator; filled cake keeps for 3 days in the refrigerator

**CHOCOLATE PRALINE
LAYER CAKE**
*Almond praline adds a
sophisticated touch to the
Chocolate Layer Cake.*

Pecan Chocolate Fudge Cake

This is a wonderfully rich, moist cake, delicious served with Crème Anglaise, vanilla ice cream, or just plain whipped cream. Be sure to serve the cake at room temperature, when the texture of the cake and its chocolate flavour will be at their best and most intense.

Eye-catching chocolate ribbons, dusted with cocoa, top this cake

INGREDIENTS

For the cake

140g (4½oz) plain chocolate
75g (2½oz) continental plain chocolate
90g (3oz) unsalted butter
5 eggs
180g (6oz) caster sugar
1 tsp vanilla extract
90g (3oz) plain flour
½ tsp salt
¾ tsp baking powder
3 tbsp soured cream or buttermilk

For the frosting and decoration

150g (5oz) pecan nuts
180g (6oz) continental plain chocolate
180g (6oz) plain chocolate
350ml (12fl oz) double cream
45g (1½oz) butter
plain, milk and white chocolate ribbons (see page 44)
cocoa powder

1 For the cake, melt both chocolates and the butter together (see page 34).

2 Put the eggs, sugar and vanilla in a large bowl set over hot water. Whisk until the eggs have doubled in volume and thickened. Stir in the chocolate mixture.

3 Sift the flour, salt and baking powder together three times. Sift the flour over the chocolate mixture, a third at a time, folding in each part carefully. Fold in the soured cream or buttermilk.

4 Pour the mixture into the prepared tin. Bake in the preheated oven for about 55 minutes, or until a skewer inserted in the centre comes out clean. Sit the cake in the tin on a wire rack for 10 minutes; turn out on to the wire rack to cool.

5 For the frosting, lightly toast the pecan nuts in the oven for about 10 minutes. Coarsely chop them.

6 Break both chocolates into a bowl. Bring the cream to the boil and pour over the chocolate. Stir gently to blend. Stir in the butter. Set aside 250ml (8fl oz) of the mixture and stir the chopped pecans into the rest. Beat both mixtures until thick enough to spread.

7 Cut the cake into three layers (see page 50) and put one layer on a thin cake board or flat serving plate. Use the pecan frosting to sandwich the layers together. Cover the top and sides of the cake with the plain frosting (see page 51). Decorate the cake with chocolate ribbons and a dusting of cocoa.

Oven temperature
160°C/325°F/gas 3

Baking time
55 minutes

Baking tin
23cm (9in) cake tin, greased, lined with greased silicone paper and floured

Makes
16 slices

Storage
Keeps for 3–4 days in the refrigerator

Freezing
1–2 months, unfilled and undecorated

Black Forest Gâteau

An impressively tempting chocolate cake layered with an irresistible combination of cherries, cream and Kirsch. Fresh cherries, with their leaves, make an attractive decoration.

INGREDIENTS

For the cake

8 eggs
200g (7oz) caster sugar
1 tsp vanilla extract
200g (7oz) continental plain chocolate
125ml (4fl oz) water
150g (5oz) plain flour, sifted

For the filling and decoration

1kg (2lb) fresh cherries, preferably morello or sour, washed and stoned
90g (3oz) granulated sugar
4 tbsp lemon juice
4 tbsp water
150ml (¼ pint) Kirsch
1.25 litres (2 pints) double cream
2 tbsp caster sugar
plain chocolate caraque (see page 43)
whole fresh cherries and leaves

1 Break the eggs into a large heatproof bowl, preferably a copper one, and gradually beat in the sugar, using an electric hand-held beater. Set the bowl over hot water and beat for 6–8 minutes, until the mixture has doubled in volume and is thick enough to leave a ribbon trail when the whisk is lifted. Beat in the vanilla extract.

2 Melt the chocolate and the water together (see page 34). Sift the flour over the egg mixture, a third at a time, folding in each batch carefully with a large metal spoon. Fold in the warm, but not hot, melted chocolate.

3 Divide the mixture evenly between the prepared tins and bake in the preheated oven for 30–35 minutes, or until a skewer inserted in the centre of the cakes comes out clean. Leave the cakes in the tins for a few minutes then slip a knife around the edges and turn them out on to a wire rack.

4 For the filling, put the cherries in a pan and add the granulated sugar, lemon juice and water. Simmer over a very low heat until the cherries have slightly softened, about 5 minutes (sour cherries will take longer). Strain and reserve the juices. Mix 75ml (2½fl oz) of the strained juice with 90ml (3fl oz) of the Kirsch and set aside.

5 Whip the cream until it forms soft peaks, beat in the caster sugar and fold in the remaining Kirsch.

TO FINISH THE CAKE

1 Cut each cake into two layers (see page 50). Put one layer on a thin cake board or flat cake plate and sprinkle with 3 tablespoons of the Kirsch syrup. Cover with a sixth of the whipped cream. Press half the cherries evenly over the cream. Put a second cake layer on top and repeat the syrup, cream and cherries layer.

2 Put a third cake layer on top, sprinkle with the remaining Kirsch syrup and spread over a layer of cream. Cover with the last cake layer and spread the top and sides with the remaining cream.

3 Complete the decoration by pressing the chocolate caraque into the cream round the sides of the cake and arranging the fresh cherries and leaves on top.

4 Chill the cake for 2–3 hours before serving in thin slices. To slice, cut with a knife heated in hot water then dried.

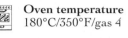

Oven temperature
180°C/350°F/gas 4

Baking time
30–35 minutes

Baking tins
Two 23cm (9in) cake tins or springform tins, greased, base-lined, then greased again and floured

Makes
12–16 slices

Storage
Keeps for 5 days in the refrigerator, unfilled and undecorated. Completed cake keeps for 3 days in the refrigerator.

Freezing
2 months, unfilled and undecorated

Fresh cherries add a perfect finishing touch

Gâteau Royale

*A class of its own!
This elegant cake is a true
classic. A light Genoese
sponge is layered with
whipped cream and there is
a rich, mousse-like
chocolate frosting to fill
and cover the cake. Lavish
rolls of chocolate waves,
strewn with gold leaf,
complete the cake's truly
royal decoration.*

INGREDIENTS

For the cake

100g (3½oz) plain flour
45g (1½oz) cocoa powder
½ tsp baking powder
⅛ tsp salt
4 eggs
150g (5oz) caster sugar
1 tsp vanilla extract
45g (1½oz) unsalted butter

For the frosting

150g (5oz) plain chocolate
3 eggs, separated
90g (3oz) unsalted butter, room temperature
1½ tsp vanilla extract
pinch of salt

For the filling and decoration

150ml (¼ pint) double cream
1 tbsp caster sugar
plain chocolate waves (see page 44)
edible gold leaf (optional)

1 Sift the flour, cocoa, baking powder and salt together three times. Set aside.

2 Break the eggs into a large heatproof bowl, preferably a copper one, and gradually beat in the sugar, using a hand-held electric beater. Set the bowl over hot water and beat for 6–8 minutes, until the mixture has doubled in volume and is thick enough to leave a ribbon trail. Whisk in the vanilla.

3 Melt the butter and set aside. Sift the dry ingredients over the egg mixture, a third at a time, folding in each batch carefully. Fold in the butter.

4 Pour the mixture into the prepared tin and bake in the preheated oven for 35–40 minutes, or until the top of the cake springs back when lightly pressed. Leave the cake in the tin for a few minutes before turning it out on to a wire rack to cool.

5 For the frosting, melt the chocolate in a medium-size bowl (see page 33). While the chocolate is still hot beat in the egg yolks, one by one. Cut the butter into small pieces and blend into the chocolate mixture. Stir in 1 teaspoon of the vanilla. Whisk the egg whites with the salt until stiff.

Oven temperature
180°C/350°F/gas 4

Baking time
35–40 minutes

Baking tin
23cm (9in) springform cake tin, greased, base-lined, then greased and floured

Makes
8–10 slices

Storage
Keeps for 2–3 days in the refrigerator

Freezing
2 months, unfilled and undecorated

Step ahead
Make the cake; keeps for 2 days, wrapped, in the refrigerator

A rich egg-based frosting covers the cake

6 Fold a large spoonful of the whites into the chocolate mixture to lighten it. Carefully fold in the remaining whites.

7 For the filling, whip the cream to soft peaks, then fold in the sugar and remaining vanilla extract.

TO FINISH THE CAKE

1 Cut the cake into 3 layers (see page 50). Put the bottom layer on a thin cake board or flat plate and spread it with a third of the frosting. Add a second cake layer and spread it with the cream. Top with the remaining cake layer.

2 Cover the top and sides of the cake with the remaining chocolate frosting. Decorate with chocolate waves and edible gold leaf, if liked.

Touches of gold glitter on top of the chocolate

GATEAU ROYALE
Imaginatively decorated, this airy cake provides a sparkling finale for a celebratory occasion.

Devil's Food Cake

This rich cake, its frosting flavoured with fruit juices, is an American classic.

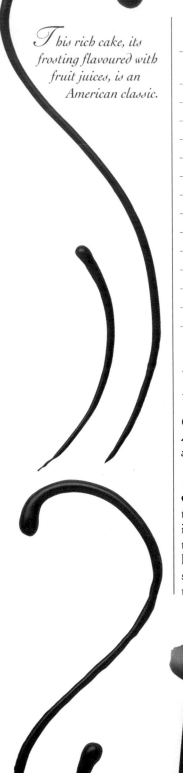

INGREDIENTS

For the cake

90g (3oz) plain chocolate, chopped (see page 32)

275g (9oz) self-raising sponge flour

1 tsp bicarbonate of soda

½ tsp salt

250g (8oz) unsalted butter, softened

400g (13oz) dark soft brown sugar

2 tsp vanilla extract

3 eggs

125ml (4fl oz) buttermilk

250ml (8fl oz) boiling water

For the frosting

300g (10oz) caster sugar

2 egg whites

1 tbsp lemon juice

3 tbsp frozen concentrated orange juice

1 Melt the chocolate (see page 33) and set aside.

2 Sift together the flour, bicarbonate of soda and salt and set aside.

3 Cream the butter until soft, add the sugar and continue to beat until light and fluffy. Stir in the vanilla extract. Beat in the eggs, one at a time, adding a little flour if the mixture starts to curdle. Stir in the chocolate.

4 Fold in the dry ingredients, a third at a time, alternating with the buttermilk. Slowly stir in the boiling water.

5 Divide the mixture evenly between the prepared tins and put them in the preheated oven so they are not directly above one another. Bake for 30 minutes, or until the tops spring back when lightly touched.

6 Cool the cakes in the tins for 5 minutes before turning out on to wire racks to cool.

7 For the frosting, put all the ingredients in the top of a double saucepan or in a bowl set over simmering water. Whisk until the mixture thickens and forms soft peaks. Remove from the heat and continue to beat until it is the right consistency for spreading (it should coat the back of a spoon).

8 Sandwich the cake layers with some of the frosting and spread the rest roughly over the top and sides of the cake with a palette knife.

Oven temperature
190°C/375°F/gas 5

Baking time
30 minutes

Baking tins
Two 23cm (9in) shallow cake tins, greased and base-lined

Makes
12–16 slices

Storage
Keeps for 2 days in the refrigerator

Freezing
Freeze unfrosted cake for 1 month

White Chocolate Cake

A plain chocolate sponge cake layered with a lightly alcoholic raspberry syrup and a rich white chocolate buttercream is the perfect choice for the lover of white chocolate.

White chocolate curls sit on white buttercream on this elegant cake

INGREDIENTS

For the cake

100g (3½oz) plain flour
45g (1½oz) cocoa powder
½ tsp baking powder
⅛ tsp salt
4 eggs
150g (5oz) caster sugar
1 tsp vanilla extract
45g (1½oz) unsalted butter

For the white chocolate buttercream

1 egg
90g (3oz) granulated sugar
50 ml (2fl oz) water
good pinch of cream of tartar
180g (6oz) unsalted butter, at room temperature
250g (8oz) white chocolate
4 tbsp water

For the raspberry syrup

125ml (4fl oz) raspberry preserve
4 tbsp Framboise (raspberry liqueur)
white chocolate curls, to decorate (see page 43)

1 Sift the flour, cocoa, baking powder and salt together three times. Set aside.

2 Break the eggs into a large heatproof bowl, preferably a copper one, and gradually beat in the sugar, using a hand-held electric beater. Set the bowl over hot water and beat for 6–8 minutes, until the mixture has doubled in volume and is thick enough to leave a ribbon trail when the whisk is lifted. Whisk in the vanilla.

3 Melt the butter over a gentle heat and set aside. Sift the dry ingredients over the egg mixture, a third at a time, folding in each batch carefully with a large metal spoon. Fold in the melted butter.

4 Pour the mixture into the prepared tin and bake in the preheated oven for 35–40 minutes, or until the cake springs back when lightly pressed. Leave the cake to rest in the tin for a few minutes. Slip a knife round the inside of the tin to loosen the cake and turn out on to a wire rack to cool.

5 For the buttercream, beat the egg until pale and thick and set aside.

6 Put the sugar, water and cream of tartar in a small saucepan. Heat gently to dissolve the sugar, then boil until the syrup reaches 115°C (240°F) on a sugar thermometer. Gradually pour the hot sugar syrup on to the egg, beating constantly. Continue beating until the mixture has cooled to room temperature.

7 Cut the butter into small pieces and beat them, a few at a time, into the egg mixture. Melt the white chocolate with the water (see page 34). When it has cooled to lukewarm stir it into the buttercream.

8 For the syrup, sieve the raspberry preserve and stir in the liqueur.

TO FINISH THE CAKE

1 Cut the cake into three layers (see page 50). Place the top layer, upside down, on a thin round cake board or flat plate. Brush with half the raspberry syrup. Spread with a quarter of the buttercream.

2 Place the second layer on top. Brush with the remaining syrup and spread with another quarter of the cream. Place the third layer on top and cover the top and sides of the cake with the remaining buttercream. Decorate the cake with large white chocolate curls.

Oven temperature
180°C/350°F/gas 4

Baking time
35–40 minutes

Baking tin
23cm (9in) springform cake tin, greased, base-lined, then greased and floured

Makes
8–10 slices

Storage
Keeps for 2–3 days in the refrigerator

Freezing
2–3 months

This is an astonishingly light and delectable flourless chocolate roulade. I have filled it with a coffee cream, but it could be filled with plain or vanilla-flavoured whipped cream. It is usual for it to crack as it is rolled up - a sign of its lightness.

Mocha Roulade

INGREDIENTS

For the cake

125g (4oz) plain chocolate
60g (2oz) continental plain chocolate
3 tbsp water
2 tbsp brandy
5 eggs, separated
180g (6oz) caster sugar
pinch of salt

For the filling and decoration

1 tsp instant espresso coffee powder
1 tbsp boiling water
300ml (½ pint) double cream
1 tsp caster sugar
plain chocolate cut-out triangles (see page 44)

1 Melt both chocolates, water and brandy together (see page 34) and set aside to cool.

2 Whisk the egg yolks with the sugar until pale in colour. Fold in the melted chocolate. Whisk the egg whites with the salt until stiff. Fold a spoonful of the whites into the yolks to lighten the mixture, then gently fold in the remaining whites.

3 Pour the mixture evenly into the prepared tin. Bake in the preheated oven for 15 minutes. Remove from the oven, cover with greaseproof paper and a damp cloth and leave for several hours, or overnight.

4 For the filling, dissolve the coffee in the water. Whip the cream to soft peaks, then fold in the coffee and caster sugar.

5 Turn the roulade out on to a sheet of greaseproof or silicone paper dusted with icing sugar. Peel off the lining paper (see step 1 below).

6 Put 3–4 tablespoons of the filling into a nylon piping bag with a 1cm (½in) nozzle. Spread the remainder over the roulade. Roll up the long side of the roulade, using the sugared paper to help (see steps 2–3, below). Discard the paper.

7 Pipe the reserved filling on top of the roulade (see page 48) and set the chocolate triangles in it. Chill the roulade for several hours before serving.

VARIATION
This roulade makes an excellent Christmas Log. Decorate it with chocolate holly leaves cut from melted chocolate or from chocolate marzipan (see pages 44 and 76) and a red berry fruit.

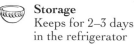

Oven temperature
180°C/350°F/gas 4

Baking time
15 minutes

Baking tin
36 x 25 x 1cm (14 x 10 x ½in) Swiss roll tin, greased and lined with silicone paper

Makes
12–16 slices

Storage
Keeps for 2–3 days in the refrigerator

Making A Roulade

1 To take the lining paper off the cold roulade, carefully lift the paper's front corners and peel it back towards you.

2 Use a palette knife with a cranked handle to spread the filling, being careful not to take it right to the edges of the roulade.

3 To prevent the roulade cracking deeply or the filling pushing out, roll it up lightly, without pressing down on it.

Coffee cream filling gives the roulade an extra piquancy

Chocolate Almond and Raspberry Roulade

An easy-to-roll sponge cake made with almonds is the basis of this roulade. It is filled with a luscious dark chocolate cream.

Mocha Roulade combines coffee and chocolate in delicious style

INGREDIENTS

For the cake

100g (3½oz) almonds
100g (3½oz) caster sugar
3 eggs
3 egg whites
pinch of salt
30g (1oz) plain flour
30g (1oz) unsalted butter, melted

For the raspberry syrup

75g (2½oz) caster sugar
90ml (3fl oz) water
5 tbsp Framboise (raspberry liqueur)

For the filling and decoration

125g (4oz) continental plain chocolate
125g (4oz) plain chocolate
125ml (4fl oz) milk
250ml (8fl oz) double cream
500g (1lb) fresh raspberries
chocolate leaves (see page 43)

1 Grind the almonds with 2 tablespoons of the sugar in a food processor or blender. Set aside 2 more tablespoons of sugar. Place the ground almonds and the remaining sugar in a large bowl. Add the eggs, one at a time, beating each egg until it is light and thick before adding the next.

2 Whisk the egg whites with the salt until stiff. Add the 2 tablespoons of sugar and whisk for 20 seconds

more, until glossy. Sift the flour over the almond mixture and carefully fold it in, using a large metal spoon. Fold in the whisked egg whites, a third at a time, and then the melted butter.

3 Turn the mixture into the prepared tin and spread it level. Bake in the preheated oven for 12–15 minutes, or until just firm. Remove the cake with its paper to a flat surface and leave until it is cool.

4 For the syrup, dissolve the sugar in the water over moderate heat, then boil until the syrup is clear. When it has cooled add the Framboise.

5 For the filling, melt the chocolates and milk together (see page 34). Whip the cream until it forms soft peaks. When the chocolate is tepid fold in a large spoonful of cream. Fold the chocolate into the rest of the cream with a large metal spoon.

TO FINISH THE ROULADE

1 Turn the cake over on to a piece of silicone or greaseproof paper and carefully peel off the lining paper (see step 1, below left). Brush the surface with the syrup. Spread with two-thirds of the chocolate cream (see step 2, below left).

2 Set aside about twelve raspberries for decoration and scatter the rest over the chocolate cream.

3 Roll up the cake from the short side, using the paper to help. Spread the remaining chocolate cream over the top and sides of the roulade. Decorate with chocolate leaves and the reserved raspberries. Keep the roulade in the refrigerator, bringing it out an hour before serving, to allow it to come to room temperature.

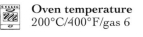 **Oven temperature**
200°C/400°F/gas 6

Baking time
12–15 minutes

Baking tin
39 x 26 x 1cm (15½ x 10½ x ½in) Swiss roll tin, greased and lined with greased silicone paper

Makes
8–10 slices

Storage
Keeps for 2–3 days in the refrigerator

Marjolaine

An elegant example of Continental patisserie, this is a meringue, made with almonds, and layered with an apricot filling and a chocolate buttercream.

INGREDIENTS

For the cake

100g (3½oz) almonds

100g (3½oz) sugar

3 eggs

3 egg whites

pinch of salt

30g (1oz) plain flour

30g (1oz) butter, melted

For the apricot filling

4 tbsp cold water

¼ tsp gelatine powder

90g (3oz) dried apricots

125ml (4fl oz) whipping cream

2 tbsp granulated sugar

For the buttercream

3 egg yolks

90g (3oz) caster sugar

75ml (2½fl oz) water

200g (7oz) unsalted butter, softened

100g (3½oz) continental plain chocolate, melted (see page 33)

cocoa powder, to decorate

---

1 For the cake, grind the almonds with 2 tablespoons of the sugar in a food processor or blender. Set aside 2 more tablespoons of sugar. Put the ground almonds and remaining sugar in a large bowl. Add the eggs, one at a time, beating each egg until it is light and thick before adding the next.

2 Whisk the egg whites with the salt until stiff. Add the 2 tablespoons sugar and whisk for 20 seconds more, until glossy. Sift the flour over the almond mixture and carefully fold in, using a large metal spoon. Fold in the egg whites, a third at a time, then the melted butter.

3 Turn the mixture into the prepared tin and spread it level. Bake in a preheated oven for 12–15 minutes, or just until firm. Remove the cake with its paper to a flat surface to cool.

4 For the apricot filling, measure the water into a cup, sprinkle over the gelatine and leave to turn spongy. Put the cup in a bowl of hot water to dissolve the gelatine. Put the apricots, cream and sugar into a saucepan and simmer for 10 minutes. Stir in the gelatine. Purée in a food processor or blender and leave to cool at room temperature.

5 For the buttercream, beat the egg yolks together in a bowl. Gently heat the sugar and water together until the sugar has dissolved, bring to the boil, and boil until the syrup reaches the soft ball stage, 115°C (240°F) on a sugar thermometer.

6 Gradually pour the syrup over the eggs, beating continually, until the mixture is cool and thick. Cream the butter and blend into the egg mixture. Mix in the melted chocolate.

TO FINISH THE CAKE

1 Turn the cake over on to a piece of greaseproof paper, and remove the lining paper. Cut the cake into four equal-sized rectangles.

2 Put one rectangle on a thin cake board or flat cake plate and spread with a quarter of the buttercream. Add a second layer and spread on the apricot filling. Add the third layer and spread it with buttercream. Put the last rectangle on top and cover the sides and top with the remaining buttercream.

3 Chill the Marjolaine until firm. Remove from the refrigerator 1 hour before serving. To decorate, sift a layer of cocoa over the top and score with a knife. Serve the cake in slices, cut with a hot, dry knife.

Oven temperature
200°C/400°F/gas 6

Baking time
12–15 minutes

Baking tin
36 x 25 x 1cm
(14 x 10 x ½in)
Swiss roll tin, lined with buttered greaseproof paper

Makes
12–16 slices

Storage
Keeps for 2–3 days in the refrigerator

Marble Pound Cake

Equal weights of butter, flour, sugar and eggs have been the formula for pound cakes for centuries. The buttery taste of this chocolate version makes it the perfect choice for serving with tea or coffee.

INGREDIENTS

125g (4oz) potato flour
125g (4oz) plain flour
1 tsp baking powder
¼ tsp salt
250g (8oz) unsalted butter, softened
250g (8oz) caster sugar
4 eggs
2 tbsp milk
1 tsp vanilla extract
90g (3oz) plain chocolate, melted
2 tbsp cocoa powder blended with 2 tbsp boiling water
½ quantity Chocolate Glaze (see page 136), to decorate

1 Sift the flours, baking powder and salt together twice and set aside.

2 Cream the butter and sugar until light and fluffy. Mix the eggs with the milk and vanilla and add very gradually to the butter mixture. Fold in the flour, a quarter at a time.

3 Spoon half the mixture into the prepared mould. Mix the melted chocolate and cocoa into the remaining mixture and spoon into the mould, swirling the mixture for a marbled effect.

4 Bake the cake in the preheated oven for 1 hour, or until firm. Leave in the mould for 10 minutes, then turn out on to a wire rack to cool.

5 Put the cooled cake on a piece of greaseproof paper. When the Chocolate Glaze has cooled to a coating consistency (it should coat the back of a spoon), pour it over the top of the cake, letting it drip down the sides. Leave to set.

Oven temperature
180°C/350°F/gas 4

Baking time
1 hour

Baking tin
1.5 litre (2½ pint) tubular cake tin, greased with melted butter and floured

Makes
12 slices

Storage
Keeps for 2–3 days in the refrigerator

Freezing
1 month

Dacquoise

This is a wonderful confection of hazelnut meringues layered with chocolate cream and topped with raspberries or strawberries. It can easily be transformed into a summer dessert by replacing the chocolate with whipped cream, mixed with fresh berry fruits.

INGREDIENTS

For the meringues

250g (8oz) hazelnuts, toasted and skinned (see page 38)
1 tbsp cornflour
300g (10oz) caster sugar
2 tbsp cocoa powder
6 egg whites

For the filling and decoration

1 quantity Chocolate Ganache (see page 136)
400g (13oz) strawberries

1 Finely grind the cooled nuts in a food processor with the cornflour and 3 tablespoons of the sugar. Tip the mixture into a bowl and stir in the cocoa.

2 Whisk 3 of the egg whites to form soft peaks. Gradually whisk in half the remaining sugar to form stiff glossy peaks. Fold in half the nut mixture.

3 Divide the mixture between the prepared baking sheets and spread out in the marked circles. Bake in the preheated oven for 1 hour, or until crisp and dry. Cool on wire racks.

4 Reline the baking sheets. Make up the remaining meringue ingredients and bake 2 more discs. When they are cold, peel off the lining papers.

5 Make the chocolate ganache according to the method on page 136.

6 Put a meringue disc on a serving plate and spread with chocolate cream. Repeat with the other discs, spreading the top one with all the remaining cream. Chill for 2 hours. Arrange the fresh strawberries over the top of the Dacquoise before serving it.

Oven temperature
140°C/275°F/gas 1

Baking time
1 hour for each batch of meringues

Baking tins
Two flat baking sheets, each lined with silicone paper or foil and marked with a 23cm (9in) circle

Makes
12 slices

Storage
Keeps for 2–3 days in the refrigerator

Wedding Cake

This plain chocolate sponge cake, iced and decorated with white chocolate, will please all chocolate-lovers. Each of the three cakes is cut into layers which are then sandwiched together with a buttercream flavoured with fresh strawberries. The combination of flavours is delicious. The sponge cakes freeze well and can be thawed out overnight at room temperature. The individually iced cakes can be assembled and decorated the day before the wedding and stored in a cool place.

The Wedding Cake slices easily and will serve up to 100 guests

INGREDIENTS

For the 30cm (12in) cake

275g (9oz) continental plain chocolate
150g (5oz) plain chocolate
225ml (7½fl oz) water
12 eggs
375g (12oz) caster sugar
290g (9½oz) plain flour, sifted

For the 23cm (9in) cake

250g (8oz) continental plain chocolate
60g (2oz) plain chocolate
125ml (4fl oz) water
7 eggs
200g (7oz) caster sugar
150g (5oz) plain flour

For the 15cm (6in) cake

150g (5oz) continental plain chocolate
6 tbsp water
5 eggs
150g (5oz) caster sugar
125g (4oz) plain flour, sifted

For the buttercream

18 egg yolks
625g (1¼lb) caster sugar
350ml (12fl oz) water
1.5kg (3lb) unsalted butter, softened
250g (8oz) strawberries

For the white chocolate icing

1.15kg (2¼lb) white chocolate, chopped into small pieces
400ml (14fl oz) double cream

For the white chocolate decoration

white chocolate ribbons and cut-out petals (see pages 44 and 45), made with 750g (1½lb) white chocolate

Make the 30cm (12in) cake first, then make the 23cm (9in) and 15cm (6in) cakes together.

1 For each cake, put the chocolate and water in a small saucepan and gently bring to the boil. Remove from the heat, stir until blended and leave to cool.

2 Break the eggs into a large (very large for the 12-egg cake) heatproof bowl and set it over a pan of hot but not boiling water. Using an electric hand-held beater, whisk the eggs with the caster sugar until the mixture has doubled in volume and is thick enough to leave a ribbon trail, about 25 minutes for the 12-egg cake, 12 minutes for the 7-egg cake and 10 minutes for the 5-egg cake.

3 Sift the flour over the egg mixture, a third at a time, folding it in carefully. Fold in the melted chocolate.

4 Pour into the prepared tin and bake in the preheated oven for the recommended time, or until a skewer inserted in the centre comes out clean. Leave the cake in the tin for a few minutes, then turn out on to a wire rack to cool.

5 For the buttercream, put the egg yolks in a large bowl and whisk until they are pale and thick. Put the sugar and water in a heavy-based saucepan. Simmer, covered, for 1 minute to dissolve the sugar. Uncover and boil until the syrup reaches 115°C (240°F) on a sugar thermometer. Gradually pour the hot sugar syrup on to the eggs (avoiding the beaters), beating constantly. Continue beating until the mixture has cooled to room temperature.

6 Cut the softened butter into small pieces and beat them into the mixture, a few at a time. Set aside a third of the buttercream. Mash the strawberries and beat them into the remaining buttercream.

7 Slice each cake into three layers. Use the strawberry buttercream to sandwich the layers together. Put each cake on the appropriate-size thin cake board and set each one on a wire rack with a large square of foil underneath.

Oven temperature
180°C/350°F/gas 4

Baking time
60–65 minutes for the 30cm (12in) cake; 40–45 minutes for the 23cm (9in) cake; 35–40 minutes for the 15cm (6in) cake

Baking tins
30 x 5cm (12 x 2in) cake tin; 23 x 5cm (9 x 2in) cake tin; 15 x 5cm (6 x 2in) cake tin, each greased, bottom-lined with greaseproof paper, then greased again and floured

To assemble the cake
35.5cm (14in) heavy cake board; 30cm (12in) thin cake board; 23cm (9in) thin cake board; 15cm (6in) thin cake board
6 acrylic cake skewers
3m (3¼ yds) of 2.5cm (1in)-wide ribbon
3½m (4 yds) of 1.5cm (¾in)-wide ribbon
stainless steel pins

Makes
100 slices

Storage
Sponge cakes keep for 3 days in the refrigerator; iced cakes keep for 3 days in the refrigerator

Freezing
Sponge cakes keep for 2 months

8 Pour a thin layer of the plain buttercream over each cake, returning to the bowl any buttercream that runs on to the foil. Chill the cakes for a few minutes to set the buttercream.

9 For the icing, melt the white chocolate carefully (see page 33). Bring the cream to a simmer, remove from the heat and leave to cool, then stir it into the chocolate.

10 Cool the icing to a spreading consistency (it should coat the back of a spoon) and pour enough over each cake to cover it, spreading the icing over the top and down the sides with a palette knife. Also put a thin layer, about 3.5cm (1½in) wide, on the top edge of the heavy cake board. If the icing becomes too cold to spread, gently reheat it over hot water. Leave the icing to set.

TO ASSEMBLE THE CAKE

1 Push the acrylic skewers into the large cake, in an even circle about 3.5cm (1½in) in from the edge; mark the point where they are level with the top of the cake and remove them. Cut the skewers to the mark and put them back in the cake. Use the cut-off pieces of the skewers to make similar supports for the middle tier.

2 Leaving the cakes on their thin boards, set the large cake in the centre of the heavy cake board, the middle-size cake on the large cake and the small cake on top.

3 Pin the wide ribbon round the heavy cake board and the narrow ribbon round the bottom edge of each cake.

Ribbons disguise the joins between the Wedding Cake's three tiers

TO DECORATE THE CAKE

Assemble 9 bunches of chocolate ribbons and petals, each with 3 ribbons and 5 petals. Arrange 4 bunches on the bottom tier, 3 on the middle tier and 2 on the top tier, holding the pieces in place with dabs of melted white chocolate made from the chocolate ribbon trimmings and spooned into a paper piping bag. Pleat pieces of the narrow ribbon and pin into the centre of each bunch.

Chocolate and real ribbons give a fairy-tale quality to the Wedding Cake

Dessert Cakes

The single-layer cakes in this section make fine dessert cakes, especially good when served with a sauce, such as crème anglaise, or a fruit coulis or syrup, like the kumquat syrup made for the Celestial Kumquat Torte on this page. Many of the cakes here are in the rich tradition of the Austrian and German torte, often enriched with nuts or seeds and containing little or no flour. The classic Sacher Torte is among such cakes here, as well as two delicious Italian cakes, combining chocolate with chestnuts or amaretti biscuits.

Celestial Kumquat Torte

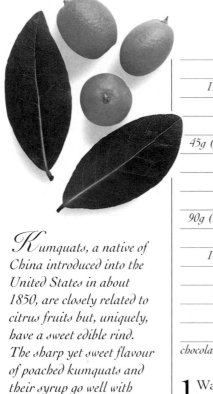

Kumquats, a native of China introduced into the United States in about 1850, are closely related to citrus fruits but, uniquely, have a sweet edible rind. The sharp yet sweet flavour of poached kumquats and their syrup go well with many chocolate desserts, including this rich torte.

INGREDIENTS

For the kumquats

500g (1lb) kumquats
150g (5oz) granulated sugar
300ml (½ pint) water

For the cake

45g (1½oz) self-raising sponge flour
150g (5oz) caster sugar
pinch of salt
3 eggs
90g (3oz) continental plain chocolate
1 tbsp cocoa powder
100g (3½oz) unsalted butter

For the glaze

125g (4oz) plain chocolate
30g (1oz) unsalted butter
2 tbsp milk
chocolate leaves, to decorate (see page 43)

1 Wash the kumquats and halve them lengthways, leaving 9–10 whole for decoration. Put in a pan with the sugar and water. Bring to the boil and cook very slowly for 30 minutes, until soft. Set aside.

2 For the cake, put the flour, sugar, salt and eggs in a large bowl set over hot but not boiling water and beat with an electric beater for about 8 minutes. The mixture should become very thick and leave a ribbon trail when the beater is lifted.

3 Melt the chocolate, cocoa powder and butter together (see page 34), add to the egg mixture and beat for a few more minutes. Pour the mixture into the prepared tin and bake in the preheated oven for 25 minutes, or until the cake is springy to the touch. Remove from the oven, run a knife around the inside edge of the tin and leave for 10 minutes before turning out on to a wire rack.

4 Melt the glaze ingredients together (see page 34). Put the cake, on the wire rack, on a plate to catch excess glaze. Cool the glaze slightly so it thickens then pour it over the warm cake, spreading it evenly with a palette knife (see page 49). Leave for 10 minutes to set.

5 Decorate the top with chocolate leaves and the whole kumquats and serve the cake lukewarm, with the remaining kumquats and syrup.

Oven temperature
160°C/325°F/gas 3

Baking time
25 minutes

Baking tin
20cm (8in) springform cake tin, greased and base-lined

Makes
8–10 slices

Storage
Keeps for 2–3 days in the refrigerator

Chocolate Hazelnut Cake

Crunchy hazelnuts help give this cake an excellent texture and flavour. Because it cuts well, the cake is a good one for packed-lunch boxes. It is also a good dessert cake, served with whipped cream or fromage frais.

INGREDIENTS

For the cake

90g (3oz) hazelnuts, toasted and skinned (see page 38)

140g (4½oz) caster sugar

90g (3oz) continental plain chocolate, chopped (see page 32)

90g (3oz) plain chocolate, chopped (see page 32)

180g (6oz) unsalted butter, cut into small pieces

4 eggs, separated

1 tsp vanilla extract

30g (1oz) plain flour

¼ tsp salt

¼ tsp cream of tartar

For the decoration

1 quantity Chocolate Glaze (see page 136)

30g (1oz) white chocolate

30g (1oz) milk chocolate

1 Grind the hazelnuts with 2 tablespoons of the sugar. Melt both chocolates with the butter (see page 34); set aside.

2 Whisk the egg yolks with 90g (3oz) of the sugar until pale and thick. Stir in the warm chocolate mixture and the vanilla. Mix the flour and salt with the hazelnuts and fold into the chocolate mixture.

3 Beat the egg whites with the cream of tartar until they form soft peaks. Add the remaining sugar and continue to beat until the whites are stiff.

4 Using a large metal spoon, fold a spoonful of the whites into the chocolate mixture to lighten it. Carefully fold in the remaining whites. Scrape the mixture into the prepared tin and bake in the preheated oven for 35–40 minutes; the centre should still be moist. Cool the cake in the tin on a wire rack. Press the top level and turn out on to a thin cake board.

5 Make the Chocolate Glaze (see page 136). Spread a quarter of the glaze over the cake to keep the crumbs in place. Chill until set. Cover with the remaining glaze (see page 49). The glaze may need warming over hot water first.

6 Melt the white and milk chocolates for decoration separately and spoon them into paper piping bags.

7 Pipe circles of the two chocolates alternately on the cake and feather them with a skewer (see page 47).

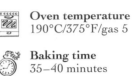 **Oven temperature**
190°C/375°F/gas 5

 **Baking time**
35–40 minutes

Baking tin
23cm (9in) springform cake tin, greased and base-lined

 Makes
10–12 slices

Storage
Keeps for 3–4 days in the refrigerator

Freezing
1–2 months

Chocolate Truffle Cake

A combination of melted chocolate and whipped cream creates this mousse-like cake, popular with today's restaurant chefs. This version has a chocolate biscuit base for added texture and crunch.

INGREDIENTS

For the biscuit base

180g (6oz) light digestive biscuits, crushed

2 tbsp cocoa powder, sifted

2 tbsp light brown sugar

75g (2½oz) unsalted butter, melted

For the filling and decoration

250g (8oz) plain chocolate

90g (3oz) continental plain chocolate

600ml (1 pint) double cream

2 tbsp milk

2 tbsp brandy or rum or 1 tsp vanilla extract

cocoa powder

white and plain chocolate piped curves (see page 47)

1 Mix together the crushed biscuits, cocoa, brown sugar and melted butter. Press in an even layer on the prepared tin's base. Bake in the preheated oven for 10 minutes.

Remove the side of the tin and put the base, with the biscuit base on it, on a wire rack to cool. When it is cool, reassemble the tin.

2 For the filling, melt the chocolates together (see page 33) and let stand until the mixture has cooled to tepid. It should still be liquid.

3 Stand the cream in its container in a bowl of hot water until it is cool but no longer refrigerator cold.

4 Whisk the cream with the milk, and brandy or vanilla, until it is thick enough to leave a ribbon trail when the whisk is lifted. Be careful not to over-whip the cream.

5 Blend a spoonful of the cream into the tepid chocolate, then quickly fold the chocolate into the rest of the cream, using a large metal spoon. Pour the mixture over the biscuit base in the tin and smooth the top with a palette knife. Cover the tin with clingfilm and chill for at least 4 hours, preferably overnight.

6 Remove the cake from the tin and leave it at room temperature for 30 minutes before serving.

7 Just before you serve the cake, sift a fine layer of cocoa powder over the top and decorate with the white and plain chocolate piped curves.

Oven temperature
180°C/350°F/gas 4

Baking time
10 minutes for the biscuit base

Baking tin
25cm (10in) springform cake tin

Makes
10–12 slices

Storage
Keeps for 3–4 days in the refrigerator

Sacher Torte

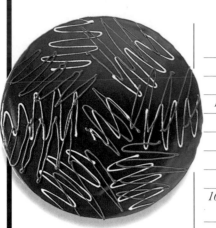

This famous cake, the original ingredients of which are still a closely guarded secret, was created in 1832 by the Austrian chef, Franz Sacher, for Prince Metternich. Later in the century, it was the subject of a seven-year legal battle over the ownership of its name. This version has a delicate chocolate flavour and a firm dark chocolate icing.

INGREDIENTS

For the cake

45g (1½oz) cocoa powder, sifted

150ml (¼ pint) boiling water

125g (4oz) unsalted butter, softened

200g (7oz) caster sugar

2 eggs, lightly beaten

1 tsp vanilla extract

½ tsp salt

165g (5½oz) self-raising sponge flour, sifted

For the chocolate glaze

125g (4oz) unsalted butter

90g (3oz) continental plain chocolate

90g (3oz) plain chocolate

1 tbsp golden syrup

For the decoration

30g (1oz) white chocolate

30g (1oz) milk chocolate

1 For the cake, whisk the sifted cocoa and water together until smooth. Set aside to cool to room temperature.

2 Beat the butter and sugar together until light and fluffy. Gradually add the eggs and vanilla. If the mixture threatens to curdle, stir in a tablespoon of the flour. Stir in the cocoa mixture and salt.

3 Sift the flour over the mixture, a third at a time, folding in each part carefully with a large metal spoon before adding the next.

4 Scrape the mixture into the prepared tin and bake in the preheated oven for 35–40 minutes, until a skewer inserted in the centre comes out clean.

5 Leave the cake to cool in the tin for 5 minutes, then turn it out on to a wire rack.

6 Melt the ingredients for the chocolate glaze together (see page 34). Sit the cake, on the wire rack, on a flat plate and pour the glaze over the top and sides, using a palette knife to spread it (see page 49).

7 For the decoration, melt the white and milk chocolates separately and spoon into paper piping bags (see page 46). Pipe zigzag lines of the chocolates over the top of the cake. Chill the cake to set the decoration.

 Oven temperature
180°C/350°F/gas 4

 Baking time
35–40 minutes

Baking tin
23cm (9in) springform cake tin, greased, floured and base-lined

Makes
10–12 slices

Storage
Keeps for 3–4 days in the refrigerator

Freezing
1–2 months

Le Diabolo

More dessert than cake, this is very luscious and richly chocolate-flavoured – an ultimate confection. To savour its full flavour and melting texture, serve it at room temperature, with a bowl of thick whipped cream on the side.

INGREDIENTS

180g (6oz) plain or bittersweet chocolate, chopped (see page 33)

180g (6oz) unsalted butter, cut into small pieces

2 tsp vanilla extract

4 eggs, separated

140g (4½oz) caster sugar

60g (2oz) ground almonds

30g (1oz) plain flour, sifted

⅛ tsp salt

⅛ tsp cream of tartar

For the decoration

cocoa powder

icing sugar

chocolate leaves (see page 43)

1 Melt the chocolate and butter together (see page 34) and stir in the vanilla.

2 Whisk the egg yolks with 90g (3oz) of the sugar until pale and thick. Stir in the warm chocolate mixture, followed by the almonds, flour and salt.

3 Beat the egg whites with the cream of tartar until they form soft peaks. Add the remaining sugar and continue to beat until the whites are stiff.

4 Fold a large spoonful of the whites into the chocolate mixture to lighten it. Carefully fold in the remaining whites.

5 Scrape the mixture into the prepared tin and bake in the preheated oven for 40 minutes, or until a wooden skewer inserted in the centre of the cake shows moist crumbs. Leave the cake in the tin on a wire rack to cool. Press the cake level before removing it from the tin.

6 To decorate the cake, dust the top with cocoa. Put leaves on the cocoa and dust icing sugar round them. Lift off the leaves and put chocolate leaves on top, arranged so that the leaf shapes, stencilled in icing sugar, also show.

Oven temperature
190°C/375°F/gas 5

Baking time
40 minutes

Baking tin
20cm (8in) springform cake tin, greased and lined

Makes
10–12 slices

Storage
Keeps for 3–4 days in the refrigerator

Amaretti Chocolate Cake

Amaretti biscuits, which have a strong almond flavour, provide the distinctive taste in this Italian chocolate cake. As it bakes, the cake settles into two layers, with the amaretti crumbs settling in the lower half of the cake.

INGREDIENTS

180g (6oz) unsalted butter

150g (5oz) caster sugar

4 eggs, separated

90g (3oz) self-raising flour, sifted

pinch of salt

90g (3oz) amaretti biscuits, crushed

125ml (4fl oz) full fat milk

60g (2oz) continental plain chocolate, finely grated (see page 42)

pinch of cream of tartar

icing sugar, to decorate

1 Cream the butter and sugar until light and fluffy. Add the egg yolks, one at a time, beating well after each addition.

2 Mix together the flour, salt and biscuits. Fold into the butter and egg mixture, a little at a time, alternating with the milk. Add the grated chocolate.

3 Whisk the egg whites with the cream of tartar until they form stiff peaks. Fold a large spoonful of the whites into the cake mixture to lighten it, then carefully fold in the remaining egg whites.

4 Pour the mixture into the prepared tin and bake in the preheated oven for 45 minutes, or until a skewer inserted in the centre comes out clean. Cool the cake on a wire rack. Remove from the tin and dust with sifted icing sugar.

Oven temperature
180°C/350°F/gas 4

Baking time
45 minutes

Baking tin
23cm (9in) springform cake tin, greased, base-lined, then greased and floured

Makes
8–10 slices

Storage
Keeps for 4–5 days in the refrigerator

Torta di Castagne e Cioccolato

This classic Italian recipe, somewhere between a dessert and a cake, is sold in cake and confectionery shops in many parts of Italy. Serve it at room temperature with a bowl of crème fraîche or creamy mascarpone cheese, and a jug of chocolate sauce.

INGREDIENTS

375g (12oz) vacuum-packed cooked and peeled chestnuts

150ml (¼ pint) milk

250g (8oz) caster sugar

5 eggs, separated

100g (3½oz) unsalted butter, softened

2 tsp vanilla extract

¼ tsp salt

100g (3½oz) continental plain chocolate

100g (3½oz) almonds

grated rind of 1 lemon

pinch of cream of tartar

icing sugar, to decorate

1 Put the chestnuts and milk in a saucepan, cover and slowly bring to the boil. Remove from the heat and set aside to cool.

2 Set 3 tablespoons of the sugar aside. In a large bowl, whisk the remaining sugar with the egg yolks. Blend in the softened butter, vanilla and salt.

3 Put the chocolate and almonds in a food processor and process until finely grated.

Stir the chocolate and nuts into the egg mixture.

4 Purée the chestnuts with the milk in a food processor and mix into the egg mixture. Stir in the lemon rind.

5 Whisk the egg whites with the cream of tartar until they form soft peaks. Gradually add the reserved sugar and whisk for 20 seconds more, or until glossy. Fold a large spoonful of the whites into the cake mixture to lighten it, then carefully fold in the remaining whites.

6 Pour the mixture into the prepared tin and bake in the preheated oven for 50 minutes, or until a skewer inserted in the centre comes out clean.

7 Set the cake on a wire rack, run a knife around the inside edge of the tin and leave for 10 minutes, then invert on to a wire rack to cool. Sift the icing sugar over the cake before serving, with a creamy cheese and a jug of chocolate sauce, if liked.

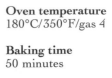

Oven temperature
180°C/350°F/gas 4

Baking time
50 minutes

Baking tin
3.5cm (1½in) deep 25cm (10in) cake tin, greased, base-lined, then greased and floured

Makes
12–16 slices

Storage
Keeps for 2–3 days in the refrigerator

Striped Cheesecake

Although this cake looks as if it must be tricky to make, it could not be easier. By spooning the light and dark mixtures one on top of the other, the circles appear as if by magic. The cheesecake's fine texture comes from using a rich, creamy cream cheese.

INGREDIENTS

For the biscuit base

225g (7½oz) digestive biscuits, finely crushed

3 tbsp cocoa powder, sifted

2 tbsp light brown soft sugar

90g (3oz) butter, melted

For the filling

750g (1½lb) cream cheese

200g (7oz) caster sugar

3 extra large eggs

150g (5 oz) plain chocolate, melted with 50 ml (2fl oz) water (see page 34)

2 tsp vanilla extract

1 For the biscuit base, put the crushed biscuits in a bowl. Stir in the cocoa and sugar.

Pour over the melted butter and toss with a fork to blend. Press the crumbs evenly into the bottom of the springform tin. (If liked, keep back 3 or 4 tablespoonfuls of the crumbs to press round the side of the baked cheesecake.)

2 Bake in the preheated oven at the higher setting for 10 minutes. Cool on a wire rack. Reduce the oven temperature to the lower setting.

3 Carefully remove the side of the springform tin from the biscuit base and lightly grease it with butter. When the biscuit base has cooled, reassemble the springform tin.

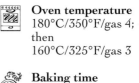

Oven temperature
180°C/350°F/gas 4; then 160°C/325°F/gas 3

Baking time
10 minutes for the base; 1 hour 10 minutes for the cheesecake

Baking tin
23 x 6cm (9 x 2½in) springform tin, only sides greased

Makes
12–14 slices

Storage
Keeps for 1 week in the refrigerator

TO MAKE THE FILLING

1 Put the cream cheese in a large bowl. Beat, using a hand-held beater or an electric mixer, until smooth. Continue to mix, gradually adding the sugar. Add the eggs, one at a time, beating only enough to combine them with the rest of the mixture.

2 Pour about half the cheese mixture into another bowl and add the warm melted chocolate and water. Add 1 teaspoon of vanilla to both the light and chocolate mixtures.

3 Pour a little less than half of the light mixture into the centre of the tin; tilt the tin so it spreads out in an even layer and covers the biscuit base (see step 1 below). Gently pour a little less than half the chocolate mixture over the centre of the light mixture and leave to spread out, without tilting the tin (see step 2 below).

4 Alternate the layers, using about half the remaining mixture each time, until both mixtures are used up, ending with the light mixture (see steps 3–4, below). You should get four pourings of the light mixture and three of the chocolate mixture.

5 Put a pan of hot water on the bottom rack of the preheated oven and the cheesecake on the rack above. Bake for 1 hour and 10 minutes, or until the light mixture in the centre is just set. The chocolate mixture will firm up when cool.

6 Remove the cake from the oven, run a knife around the inside edge to release the cake from the tin. Set the cheesecake, in the tin, on a wire rack to cool.

7 Carefully remove the side of the tin. Chill the cheesecake until cold. Slide a palette knife between the bottom of the tin and the biscuit base and remove the cheesecake to a serving plate. Leave the cheesecake at room temperature for an hour before serving.

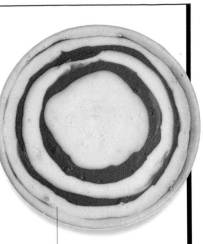

Simple stripes make an impressive decoration for the cheesecake

How to make the cheesecake

1 *Pour about half the light mixture into the tin, tilting it a little to help the mixture spread over the biscuit base.*

2 *Add the first chocolate stripe carefully into the centre of the light layer. As it settles, it pushes the light layer outwards.*

3 *Use a cup to pour in successive layers of mixture: this ensures you have control over the amount added each time.*

4 *The final pouring should be of the light mixture. The tin will be filled to within 2.5cm (1in) of the top.*

The stripes go through the cheesecake

Valentine's Day Cake

What better way of expressing your love on Valentine's Day than to share this gorgeous, rose-decorated, heart-shaped chocolate cake with your beloved?

Roses and leaves moulded from chocolate marzipan decorate the cake

INGREDIENTS

For the cake

1 quantity Le Diabolo (see page 73)

For the chocolate marzipan

2 tbsp cocoa powder

4–5 tsp boiling water

875g (1¾lb) white marzipan

For the decoration

3 tbsp apricot jam, melted with 1 tbsp water and sieved (apricot glaze)

4 chocolate marzipan roses (see page 48) and 14 leaves (see below)

2m (2 yards) of 1cm (½in)-wide ribbon

1 Make the Le Diabolo mixture and put it into the prepared tin. Bake in the preheated oven for about 1 hour, or until a skewer inserted in the centre comes out clean.

2 Put the cake, in the tin, on a wire rack to cool completely. Remove the cake from the tin and peel off the baking paper.

3 For the chocolate marzipan, blend the cocoa with enough boiling water to make a smooth, stiff paste. Allow it to cool, then knead it into the marzipan until the marzipan is smoothly chocolate-coloured throughout. If the marzipan is not to be used immediately, wrap it in clingfilm and store in a cool place.

TO ASSEMBLE THE CAKE

1 Put the cake on the cake board and brush it all over with the warm apricot glaze.

2 Set aside one third of the marzipan. Roll out the rest on a surface lightly dusted with cocoa to a circular shape about 26cm (10½in) across.

3 Carefully pick up the marzipan, supported on the rolling pin, and lay it over the cake. Dust your fingers with a little cocoa powder and smooth the marzipan gently over the top and down the sides of the cake.

4 Trim the marzipan neatly round the bottom edge of the cake. Set the trimmings aside.

5 Take about two-thirds of the remaining piece of marzipan and roll it out very thinly on a surface lightly dusted with cocoa to a size large enough to cover the top of the cakeboard.

6 Carefully lift the cake off the board and put it to one side. Using the rolling pin, lift the marzipan on to the board and smooth it over. Trim the marzipan round the top edge of the board. Keep the trimmings for the decorations.

7 Spread a little apricot glaze over the centre of the marzipan-covered board and put the cake back in place.

TO MAKE AND ARRANGE THE DECORATIONS

1 Knead together the leftover marzipan and trimmings. Use to make moulded roses (see page 48) and leaves. To make marzipan leaves, press a small clean rose leaf on to thinly rolled-out marzipan, run a knife round the edge of the leaf then lift it off the marzipan. Shape the leaf into a curve over your fingers. Put the roses and leaves in a warm, dry place to firm up (being made of marzipan, they will not dry hard).

2 Arrange the roses and leaves on the cake, pressing them gently into place. Fix the ribbon round the bottom edge of the cake and round the edge of the cake board, using stainless-steel pins to secure it in place.

Oven temperature
180°C/350°F/gas 4

Baking time
About 1 hour

Baking equipment
20cm (8in) heart-shaped cake tin, greased and lined with silicone paper; 25cm (10in) heart-shaped thick cake board

Makes
16–20 slices

Storage
Keeps for 2–3 days in the refrigerator

Step ahead
Make the apricot glaze a day ahead; make the chocolate marzipan a few hours beforehand

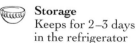

VALENTINE'S DAY CAKE *There is double chocolate enjoyment in this romantic, rose-covered cake, for beneath the rich chocolate marzipan covering is a luscious chocolate and almond cake.*

Roses bring true romance to a special cake

Teatime Chocolate

Homemade squares and small cakes are always greatly appreciated, few more so than the Brownies, which open this section. They are among the easiest of squares to bake and there are many variations on the basic recipe. Other recipes here with the same virtues of being quick to make and delicious to eat are Chocolate Muffins and Bishop's Bread, a splendid chocolate teabread. Other favourites here are the choux pastry treats, Eclairs and Profiteroles, and meringues have been given the full chocolate treatment, too.

Swirls of chocolate: Marbled Brownies ready to cut into squares

Brownies

There must be hundreds of recipes for Brownies and this is one of the best. It has the added virtue of being quick to make. There is an easily made marbled variation, too, in which the walnuts are replaced by cream cheese.

INGREDIENTS

125g (4oz) lightly salted butter

45g (1½oz) cocoa powder

2 eggs

250g (8oz) caster sugar

60g (2oz) self-raising flour

90g (3oz) walnuts

1 Gently melt the butter in a small, heavy-based saucepan, then stir in the cocoa until blended and set aside.

2 Beat the eggs until light and fluffy. Gradually add the sugar and stir in the chocolate mixture. Sift the flour over the top and fold it into the mixture. Fold in the nuts.

3 Pour the mixture into the prepared tin and bake in the preheated oven for 30–35 minutes, or until just cooked through and springy to the touch. Brownies are at their best when moist, so be careful not to overbake them.

4 Cool the baked cake in the tin. Turn it out and cut into squares. If liked, melt 60g (2oz) plain chocolate (see page 32) and spread over the cooled cake before cutting it into squares.

VARIATION
Marbled Brownies
For these, make the Brownies recipe to the end of step 2, replacing the walnuts with 1 teaspoon vanilla extract.

For the "marbling", whisk together 180g (6oz) cream cheese, 1 egg and 90g (3oz) caster sugar; sift 30g (1oz) self-raising flour over this mixture and fold in. Add 1 teaspoon of vanilla extract.

Pour three-quarters of the basic brownies mixture into the prepared tin and spread the cream cheese mixture over it. Drop spoonfuls of the remaining mixture on top, making swirls in it with a knife for a marbled effect. Bake for 35–40 minutes, or until the top is springy to the touch.

Oven temperature
180°C/350°F/gas 4

Baking time
30–35 minutes

Baking tin
20cm (8in) square cake tin, base-lined

Makes
16 squares

Storage
Keep for 3–4 days in the refrigerator

Freezing
1–2 months, un-iced

Marbled Brownie

Blonde Brownies

These are a less rich version of the classic brownie, with a caramel flavour. Like all brownies, they firm up as they cool, so be careful not to overbake them. Cooling them in the tin helps keep them moist.

INGREDIENTS

75g (2½oz) granulated sugar

2 tbsp water

180g (6oz) unsalted butter

180g (6oz) light brown sugar

2 eggs, lightly beaten

200g (7oz) self-raising flour, sifted

⅛ tsp salt

90g (3oz) walnuts, chopped

90g (3oz) plain chocolate, chopped into pea-size pieces (see page 32)

1 Heat the granulated sugar gently in a small, heavy-based saucepan until the sugar melts and caramelizes. Swirl the pan when the sugar colours and take it off the heat when it goes a dark caramel colour. Add the water to the caramel at arm's length to avoid splashes.

2 Cream the butter, then beat in the brown sugar until the mixture is light and fluffy. Gradually add the eggs to the creamed ingredients. Stir in the caramel, heating gently to thin it if it has become too thick to pour readily.

3 Sift the flour and salt together and fold into the mixture. Fold in the walnuts and chocolate.

4 Turn the mixture into the prepared tin. Bake in the preheated oven for 40–45 minutes, or until a skewer inserted into the centre comes out clean. Run a knife around the inside of the tin and leave the cake to cool for 10 minutes. Turn out and cut into squares.

Oven temperature
180°C/350°F/gas 4

Baking time
40–45 minutes

Baking tin
20cm (8in) square cake tin, base-lined

Makes
16 squares

Storage
Keep for 3–4 days in an airtight container

Freezing
2 months

Chocolate Muffins

A light-textured chocolate muffin with a surprise hidden inside. Delicious served with vanilla ice cream.

INGREDIENTS

125g (4oz) unsalted butter

90g (3oz) granulated sugar

30g (1oz) dark brown sugar

2 eggs

1 tsp vanilla extract

200g (7oz) self-raising sponge flour or self-raising flour

15g (½oz) cocoa powder

¼ tsp salt

150ml (¼ pint) milk

60g (2oz) plain chocolate, cut into 1cm (½in) pieces

1 Cream the butter, beat in both sugars and mix until the consistency is light and fluffy. Lightly mix the eggs and vanilla and gradually beat them into the creamed ingredients.

2 Sift the flour, cocoa and salt together twice. Fold the dry ingredients into the butter mixture, alternating with the milk.

3 Half-fill the paper cases in the patty tin with the mixture. Put a few pieces of chocolate on top and cover with a spoonful of the mixture. Half-fill any empty wells in the tin with water to help ensure even baking.

4 Bake in the preheated oven for about 20 minutes, or until the muffins have risen and are springy to the touch. Remove from the patty tin and cool on a wire rack. The muffins are at their best when freshly baked.

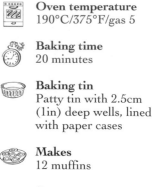

Oven temperature
190°C/375°F/gas 5

Baking time
20 minutes

Baking tin
Patty tin with 2.5cm (1in) deep wells, lined with paper cases

Makes
12 muffins

Storage
Keep for 3–4 days in an airtight container, though they are best eaten fresh.

Fudge Fingers

These fudge bars can be stirred up in a minute and make a rich treat to serve with coffee or as a snack.

INGREDIENTS

75g (2½oz) hazelnuts, toasted and skinned (see page 38)

300g (10oz) plain chocolate

150g (5oz) unsalted butter

¼ tsp salt

150g (5oz) digestive biscuits

1 Roughly chop the toasted and skinned hazelnuts.

2 Carefully melt the chocolate, butter and salt together over very low heat or in the top of a double saucepan (see page 32). Cut the biscuits into 1cm (½in) pieces. Mix the biscuits and nuts into the chocolate.

3 Turn the mixture into the prepared tin and press it into a smooth layer. Chill for at least 2 hours before cutting into fingers.

VARIATION
Replace the hazelnuts with a mixture of walnuts or almonds and raisins, chopped peel or crystallized ginger.

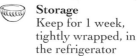

Baking tin
18cm (7in) square tin lined with silicone paper

Makes
14 fingers

Storage
Keep for 1 week, tightly wrapped, in the refrigerator

Bishop's Bread

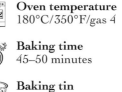

Chocolate, lemon and nuts enhance the flavour of this moist, buttery teabread.

INGREDIENTS

100g (3½oz) self-raising flour
30g (1oz) cornflour
¼ tsp baking powder
140g (4½oz) lightly salted butter
140g (4½oz) caster sugar
2 eggs
1 tsp vanilla extract
30g (1oz) sultanas
30g (1oz) walnuts, chopped
grated zest of ½ lemon
40g (1½oz) plain chocolate, chopped into pea-size pieces (see page 32)
icing sugar to decorate

1 Sift the flour, cornflour and baking powder together three times.

2 Cream the butter and sugar together until light and fluffy. Lightly mix the eggs and vanilla extract together and gradually beat them into the creamed ingredients.

3 Carefully fold the dry ingredients into the mixture, a third at a time, using a large metal spoon. Be careful not to overmix. Fold in the sultanas, walnuts, lemon zest and chocolate.

4 Pour the mixture into the prepared tin and bake in the centre of the preheated oven for 45–50 minutes, or until a skewer inserted in the centre comes out clean.

5 Cool the cake in the tin for 5 minutes before turning out on to a wire rack to finish cooling. Dust the cake with icing sugar before serving.

Oven temperature
180°C/350°F/gas 4

Baking time
45–50 minutes

Baking tin
500g (1lb) loaf tin, greased and base-lined

Makes
10 slices

Storage
Keeps for 4–5 days in an airtight container

Freezing
1–2 months

Chocolate-dipped Meringues

Meringues are versatile and easy to make – both basic white meringues and the chocolate-flavoured variation I have included here. They can be served with ice cream or summer berries, or filled with different-flavoured creams.

INGREDIENTS

4 egg whites
pinch of cream of tartar
200g (7oz) caster sugar
150g (5oz) plain chocolate, melted (see page 33)
250ml (8fl oz) double cream

1 Whisk the egg whites with the cream of tartar until they form soft peaks. Whisk in the sugar, a few tablespoons at a time, until the meringue mixture is very stiff.

2 Take up spoonfuls of the mixture and use a second spoon to push them in oval shapes on to the prepared baking sheets, leaving 2cm (¾in) spaces between each to allow for spreading. You should get about 36 meringues.

3 Bake in the preheated oven for 1 hour. Turn off the oven and leave the meringues inside until cool. Carefully peel them off the silicone paper.

4 Melt the chocolate (see page 33). Dip the bottom of each meringue shell in chocolate and put them, dipped side down, on silicone paper to set.

5 Whip the cream until it forms soft peaks. Sandwich the meringues together in pairs with the cream and place them on their sides in paper cases.

VARIATION
Chocolate Meringues
Sift 2½ tablespoons cocoa powder over the meringue mixture and fold it in, with ½ teaspoon vanilla extract. Spoon the mixture on to prepared baking sheets and bake as for the basic meringues. The mixture could also be piped from a nylon piping bag fitted with a medium nozzle.

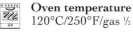

Oven temperature
120°C/250°F/gas ½

Baking time
1 hour

Baking tins
Two baking sheets lined with silicone paper

Makes
18 double meringues

Storage
Undipped and unfilled meringues keep for 1–2 months in an airtight container

Profiteroles

Profiteroles are always a welcome treat. Fill them with ice cream or a flavoured whipped cream, like the coffee cream I suggest here.

INGREDIENTS

For the choux pastry

100g (3½oz) strong plain flour
75g (2½oz) unsalted butter, cut into small pieces
175ml (6fl oz) water
½ tsp salt
2–3 eggs

For the coffee cream filling

300ml (½ pint) double cream
2 tbsp caster sugar
2 tsp instant coffee dissolved in 2 tbsp hot water

For the chocolate sauce

90ml (3fl oz) water
30g (1oz) butter
150g (5oz) plain chocolate, chopped (see page 32)
2 tbsp Grand Marnier

1 Sift the flour on to a square of greaseproof paper.

2 Put the butter, water and salt in a saucepan and bring to the boil. Off the heat, tip the flour all at once into the pan and beat it in at once, using a wooden spoon. Continue to beat over a very low heat until the mixture is smooth and pulls away from the sides of the pan (see steps 1–2 below).

3 Take off the heat, cool slightly and gradually beat in two of the eggs, mixing each addition in well before adding the next. Add only enough of the third egg to make a mixture that just falls from the spoon (see steps 3– 4, below).

4 Spoon the mixture into a pastry bag fitted with a 1cm (½in) plain nozzle. Pipe small mounds of mixture 5cm (2in) apart on to the prepared baking sheet. Bake in the preheated oven for 20–25 minutes, or until crisp. Pierce the bottom of each shell with a skewer. Turn off the oven and return the profiteroles to it for 5 minutes, leaving the oven door ajar.

5 For the coffee cream filling, whip the cream with the other ingredients. Halve the profiteroles horizontally and spoon some cream into the bottom half of each shell.

6 For the chocolate sauce, bring the water and butter to the boil, take off the heat and stir in the chocolate and liqueur. The sauce can be served hot or cold, with the profiteroles or separately in a jug.

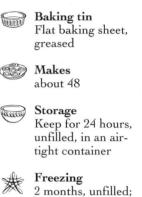

Oven temperature
200°C/400°F/gas 6

Baking time
20–25 minutes

Baking tin
Flat baking sheet, greased

Makes
about 48

Storage
Keep for 24 hours, unfilled, in an air-tight container

Freezing
2 months, unfilled; thaw, then heat in oven preheated to 180°C/350°F/gas 4 for a few minutes to restore crispness

How to make choux pastry

1 *Sift the flour on to a square of greaseproof paper. Melt the butter, water and salt in a heavy-based saucepan and bring to a fast, rolling boil.*

2 *Take the pan off the heat and tip in the flour. Over a low heat, beat the mixture rapidly with a wooden spoon to form a smooth paste that leaves the sides of the pan cleanly .*

3 *Begin beating two of the eggs into the cooled mixture, a little at a time and beating in each addition thoroughly, until the mixture is smooth and glossy.*

Éclairs

The delectable combination of crisp light choux pastry covered in chocolate and filled with a vanilla-flavoured cream ensures the continuing popularity of this classic.

INGREDIENTS

For the choux pastry

1 quantity choux pastry (see Profiteroles, opposite)

For the chocolate icing

30g (1oz) cocoa powder

30g (1oz) caster sugar

5 tbsp water

180g (6oz) icing sugar

For the crème pâtissière

500ml (17fl oz) milk

vanilla pod, split in two

6 egg yolks

125g (4oz) granulated sugar

50g (1²/₃oz) plain flour, sifted

1 Make the choux pastry as for Profiteroles. Spoon into a piping bag fitted with a 1cm (½in) plain nozzle. Pipe twelve 7cm (3in) strips of the pastry mixture, spaced well apart, on to the prepared baking sheet.

2 Bake in the preheated oven for 20–25 minutes until crisp and dry. Slice the éclairs horizontally in half while still warm to release the steam. Put on a wire rack to cool.

3 For the chocolate glaze, put the cocoa, caster sugar and water in a small saucepan and bring to the boil, stirring continuously.

4 Beat in only enough of the third egg, which will probably just be half of it, to make a mixture that falls reluctantly off the spoon. Any leftover egg could be used for glazing.

Piping choux pastry on to a baking sheet

Remove from the heat and sift in the icing sugar, stirring until smoothly blended.

4 Dip the tops of the éclairs into the glaze while it is still warm. Leave on a wire rack to set, chocolate side up.

FOR CREME PATISSIERE

1 For the crème pâtissière, bring the milk and vanilla pod to the boil. Remove from the heat, cover, and leave for 15 minutes to infuse.

2 Beat the egg yolks and sugar until thick and light, then stir in the flour. Remove the pod from the milk and return the milk to the boil. (The pod could be dried and put in a jar of sugar, for vanilla sugar, if liked.)

3 Off the heat, whisk in the egg mixture; return to a low heat and continue to cook, whisking, until the mixture thickens. Simmer for at least 5 minutes to ensure the flour loses its uncooked taste.

4 Put clingfilm on the surface to prevent a skin forming and set aside to cool. Spoon the cooled cream into the bottom half of each éclair. Replace the tops and serve the éclairs as soon as possible.

Oven temperature
200°C/400°F/gas 6

Baking time
20–25 minutes

Baking tin
Flat baking sheet, greased

Makes
12

Storage
Best eaten as soon as made

Pile profiteroles in a pyramid and serve them with a chocolate sauce

Biscuits

Among these hard-to-resist biscuits and cookies are the elegant Florentine, a luxury version of the brandy snap, and the American favourite, Toll House Cookie. There is also a chocolate version of Italy's popular biscotti, which is perfect for dunking in coffee or dessert wine. Biscuits can be time-consuming to make, but planning ahead and having all ingredients at room temperature greatly cuts the time needed. They keep well, too, so it can save time to bake a double batch or two different biscuits in one session.

— *Florentines* —

Despite their delicate appearance, these special biscuits are not at all difficult to make. They can be coated in white or milk chocolate as well as the more traditional plain chocolate. Lines of leftover melted chocolate can be drizzled over for an eye-catching extra decoration.

INGREDIENTS

For the biscuits

45g (1½oz) lightly salted butter
5 tbsp double cream
60g (2oz) caster sugar
30g (1oz) hazelnuts
30g (1oz) flaked almonds
45g (1½oz) mixed peel and chopped glacé cherries, mixed
30g (1oz) plain flour
pinch of salt

For the topping

60g (2oz) white chocolate
60g (2oz) plain chocolate

1 Melt the butter, cream and sugar together in a saucepan and slowly bring to boiling point. Remove the pan from the heat and add the hazelnuts, almonds, mixed peel and glacé cherries. When well mixed in, stir in the flour and salt.

2 Drop rounded teaspoons of the mixture 7cm (3in) apart on to the prepared baking sheets. Flatten with a wet fork.

3 Bake in the preheated oven for about 10 minutes, or until the edges are golden brown. For more perfect rounds, quickly gather the edges inside a 7cm (3in) biscuit cutter. Leave the biscuits to cool on the baking sheets for 5 minutes until firm, then carefully remove to a wire rack to cool completely.

4 Melt the chocolates for the topping separately (see page 33). Spread the undersides of the biscuits with one of the chocolates and leave to set, chocolate-side up, on a wire rack. Before the chocolate has fully set, mark wavy lines on it with a fork or confectioner's comb. Drizzle lines of leftover chocolate over the biscuits.

Oven temperature
180°C/350°F/gas 4

Baking time
10 minutes

Baking tins
Two flat baking sheets, greased

Makes
24

Storage
Keep for 1 week in an airtight container

HOME-BAKED BISCUITS
The freshly baked biscuits which fill this jar are all easy to make and are so delicious they will be quickly eaten. Make two or three of them in one baking session.

Florentines (opposite)

Pinwheel Cookies (See page 88.)

Toll House Cookies (See page 86.)

Toll House Cookies

These are all-time American favourites and justifiably so. Almost every baker in the United States has its own version of these irresistible cookies. This is one of the best; for a thinner, crisper biscuit, add 2–3 tablespoons water to the mixture.

INGREDIENTS

125g (4oz) butter

45g (1½oz) vanilla caster sugar

90g (3oz) dark brown sugar

1 egg

1 tsp vanilla extract

125g (4oz) plain flour

½ tsp bicarbonate of soda

½ tsp salt

125g (4oz) plain chocolate, chopped into pea-size pieces (see page 32)

60g (2oz) walnuts, chopped

1 Cream the butter, beat in the two sugars and mix until the consistency is light and fluffy. Lightly mix the egg and vanilla and gradually beat them into the creamed ingredients.

2 Sift the flour, bicarbonate of soda and salt together and fold into the mixture. Stir in the chopped chocolate and nuts.

3 Spoon heaped teaspoons of the mixture on to the prepared baking sheets, spaced well apart to give the cookies room to spread.

4 Bake the cookies in batches in the preheated oven for 10–12 minutes, until lightly browned. Transfer to a wire rack to cool.

Oven temperature
180°C/350°F/gas 4

Baking time
10–12 minutes per batch

Baking tins
Two or three flat baking sheets, greased

Makes
about 30

Storage
Keep for 1 week in an airtight container

White Chocolate Chip Cookies

A variation of the Toll House Cookies above, these butterscotch-flavoured crisp cookies are enriched with nuggets of white chocolate.

INGREDIENTS

125g (4oz) unsalted butter

60g (2oz) light brown sugar

75g (2½oz) dark brown sugar

1 egg

1 tsp vanilla extract

180g (6oz) plain flour

½ tsp bicarbonate of soda

½ tsp salt

150g (5oz) white chocolate, chopped into pea-size pieces (see page 32)

60g (2oz) pecan nuts, chopped

1 Cream the butter, beat in the two sugars and mix until the mixture is light and fluffy. Lightly mix the egg and vanilla and gradually beat them into the creamed ingredients.

2 Sift the flour with the bicarbonate of soda and salt and fold into the mixture. Stir in the chocolate and nuts.

3 Form the dough into 3.5cm (1½in) balls and put on the prepared baking sheets, 2.5cm (1in) apart. Flatten them with the palm of your hand.

4 Bake in the preheated oven for 10–12 minutes. Cool on the baking sheets for a few minutes then remove to a wire rack to cool completely.

Oven temperature
180°C/350°F/gas 4

Baking time
10–12 minutes

Baking tins
Two flat baking sheets, lined with silicone paper

Makes
18

Storage
Keep for 1 week in an airtight container

Chocolate Chip Peanut Butter Cookies

Children enjoy these cookies. The addition of peanut butter gives them a crumbly texture and plenty of flavour.

INGREDIENTS

125g (4oz) unsalted butter

90g (3oz) dark brown sugar

125g (4oz) crunchy peanut butter

1 egg

1 tsp vanilla extract

180g (6oz) plain flour

½ tsp bicarbonate of soda

½ tsp salt

125g (4oz) plain chocolate, chopped into pea-size pieces (see page 32)

1 Cream the butter and sugar together until the mixture is light and fluffy. Blend in the peanut butter. Lightly mix the egg and vanilla together and gradually beat into the creamed ingredients.

2 Sift the flour with the bicarbonate of soda and salt and fold into the mixture. Stir in the chopped chocolate.

3 Put heaped teaspoons of the mixture 3.5cm (1½in) apart on the prepared baking sheets and flatten them with a wet spoon. Bake in the preheated oven for 10–12 minutes. Cool on a wire rack.

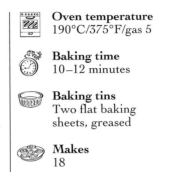

Oven temperature
190°C/375°F/gas 5

Baking time
10–12 minutes

Baking tins
Two flat baking sheets, greased

Makes
18

Storage
Keep for 1 week in an airtight container

Mocha Biscuits

A very rich, irresistible biscuit that is crisp on the outside with a meltingly moist interior.

INGREDIENTS

325g (11oz) plain chocolate, coarsely chopped (see page 32)

125g (4oz) unsalted butter

90g (3oz) plain flour

½ tsp baking powder

½ tsp salt

4 eggs

225g (7½oz) caster sugar

1 tbsp instant espresso coffee powder

2 tsp vanilla extract

200g (7oz) plain chocolate chips

1 Melt the chocolate and butter together over gentle heat (see page 34). Set aside to cool.

2 Sift the flour, baking powder and salt together.

3 Beat the eggs and sugar until pale and thick. Add the coffee powder and vanilla extract. Stir in the melted chocolate. Fold in the flour mixture, then add the chocolate chips. Leave the mixture in a cool place for 15 minutes.

4 Put level tablespoonfuls of the dough on the prepared baking sheets 5cm (2in) apart to allow the biscuits to spread.

5 Bake the biscuits in batches in the preheated oven for 10–12 minutes, or until the biscuits are shiny and cracked on top. Leave the biscuits on the baking sheets until cool, then remove to a wire rack.

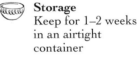

Oven temperature
180°C/350°F/gas 4

Baking time
10–12 minutes per batch

Baking tins
Two or three flat baking sheets, lined with silicone paper

Makes
32

Storage
Keep for 1–2 weeks in an airtight container

Chocolate Shortbread

These shortbreads have a melt-in-the-mouth lightness. They make an elegant accompaniment to fruit salad or ice cream.

INGREDIENTS

For the biscuits

90g (3oz) caster sugar

225g (7½oz) plain flour, sifted

pinch of salt

45g (1½oz) cocoa powder, sifted

250g (8oz) unsalted butter, cut into pea-size pieces

For the decoration

125g (4oz) plain chocolate

30g (1oz) white chocolate

1 For the biscuits, mix the caster sugar, flour, salt and cocoa powder in a bowl. Add the butter and rub in with the fingertips to form a dough.

2 Put the dough on a lightly floured surface and roll it out to 5mm (¼in) thick. Cut out biscuits with a 5cm (2in) heart-shaped cutter (or other shape, if liked). Put the biscuits on the prepared baking sheets, ensuring they do not touch each other, and chill for 1 hour.

3 Bake in the preheated oven for about 45 minutes, or until firm. Cool on the baking sheets for a few minutes before removing them to a wire rack to cool completely.

4 For the decoration, melt the chocolates separately. Put the melted white chocolate into a paper piping bag, snipping a very tiny hole in the point.

5 Spread plain chocolate over the biscuits. Before it has set, pipe the white chocolate over the biscuits, in lines for a feathered pattern, or swirls for a marbled pattern (see page 47). Leave the chocolate to set.

Oven temperature
120°C/ 250°F/gas ½

Baking time
45 minutes

Baking tins
Two flat baking sheets, lined with silicone paper

Makes
36 small shortbreads

Storage
Keep for 1 week, un-iced, in an airtight container

Pinwheel Cookies

The dough for these cookies, and the variation I suggest, will keep for 2 weeks in the refrigerator ready to be sliced and baked into fresh cookies at a moment's notice.

INGREDIENTS

375g (12oz) plain flour

200g (7oz) lightly salted butter

250g (8oz) caster sugar

2 eggs

pinch of salt

1 tsp vanilla extract

30g (1oz) plain chocolate, melted (see page 33)

1 Sift the flour and set aside.

2 Cream the butter, then beat in the sugar until light and fluffy. Lightly beat the eggs with the salt and vanilla extract and gradually add to the creamed mixture. Stir in the sifted flour.

3 Divide the dough in half. Knead the melted chocolate into half the dough. Wrap the doughs separately and chill for 30 minutes.

4 Roll the doughs, between sheets of clingfilm, into oblongs about 7cm (3in) wide and 5mm (¼in) thick. Put the dark dough on top of the light dough and roll up like a Swiss roll. Wrap tightly and chill for 4 hours, or freeze for 1 hour.

5 Cut the firm roll of dough into 6mm (⅜in) slices. Put them on the prepared baking sheets and bake in batches in the preheated oven for 8–10 minutes. While still hot, remove them to a flat surface or wire rack to cool.

VARIATION
Butterscotch Cookies
Substitute 250g (8oz) soft dark brown sugar for the caster sugar; omit the chocolate. Leave the dough in one piece. Roll out into an oblong 7cm (3in) wide and 1cm (½in) thick. Roll up the dough and make the biscuits as in steps 4 and 5 above.

Oven temperature
190°C/375°F/gas 5

Baking time
8–10 minutes per batch

Baking tins
Two or three flat baking sheets, greased

Makes
36

Storage
Keep for 2 weeks in an airtight container

Chocolate Hazelnut Tuiles

These thin tuiles can be shaped into containers to hold fruits or ice cream. Make them even more chocolate-flavoured by piping patterns of melted chocolate on them.

INGREDIENTS

90g (3oz) hazelnuts, toasted (see page 38)

100g (3½oz) caster sugar

60g (2oz) lightly salted butter

5 tsp cocoa powder

3 tbsp double cream

2 tbsp rum

2 large egg whites

45g (1½oz) plain flour

30g (1oz) plain chocolate, to decorate

1 Chop a third of the hazelnuts and set aside. Finely grind the remaining nuts and the sugar together.

2 Cream the butter, then stir in the nut/sugar mixture, cocoa, cream and rum. Add the egg whites, stirring only enough to blend. Sift the flour over the mixture and fold in.

3 Mark 4 or 5 circles, 11cm (4½in) in diameter, 5cm (2in) apart, on the prepared baking sheets. Put a scant tablespoon of the mixture in the centre of each circle and spread it out thinly with the back of the spoon. Sprinkle on a few pieces of the reserved chopped nuts.

4 Bake each batch separately in the preheated oven for about 5 minutes, or until the edges of the tuiles are just beginning to darken.

5 Remove the tuiles with a palette knife and, working quickly, put them over a rolling pin (or in a cup, if you want tuile baskets, or round a metal or paper horn). Set the baking sheet in the open oven to keep the tuiles warm and pliable.

6 Melt the plain chocolate (see page 33) and spoon into a paper piping bag (see page 46). Pipe patterns of chocolate on the cold and crisp tuiles.

Oven temperature
220°C/425°F/gas 7

Baking time
5 minutes per batch

Baking tins
Two flat baking sheets, greased with butter and floured

Makes
16

Storage
Keep for 1 week in an airtight container

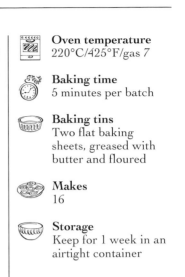

Coconut Macaroons

A chewy coconut chocolate treat. Here, I have half-dipped the macaroons in plain or white chocolate, then piped lines of the contrasting colour over them. You could also simply dip the bottoms in melted chocolate, as for the Chocolate-dipped Meringues (see page 81).

INGREDIENTS

125g (4oz) continental plain chocolate
2 egg whites
pinch of salt
100g (3½oz) granulated sugar
180g (6oz) desiccated coconut
1 tsp vanilla extract
60g (2oz) each plain and white chocolate, to decorate

1 Melt the chocolate (see page 33) and set aside to cool.

2 Whisk the egg whites with the salt until they form soft peaks. Add 3–4 tablespoons of the sugar and whisk until the mixture is glossy and firm. Fold in the remaining sugar, then the chocolate, followed by the coconut and vanilla extract.

3 Place rounded spoonfuls of the mixture 2.5cm (1in) apart on the prepared baking sheets. Bake in the preheated oven for 15–18 minutes, until the macaroons are dry on the outside but soft in the centre.

4 Melt the chocolates for the decoration separately (see page 33). Half-dip the biscuits into one or other chocolate. Lay on silicone paper to set.

5 Spoon the remaining chocolate into paper piping bags and pipe contrasting lines over the macaroons.

Oven temperature
150°C/300°F/gas 2

Baking time
15–18 minutes

Baking tins
Two flat baking sheets, lined with silicone paper

Makes
24

Storage
Keep for 4–5 days in an airtight container

Chocolate Macaroons

These delicate macaroons are crisp on the outside with a soft interior. They can be sandwiched together with raspberry jam or Chocolate Ganache (see page 136).

INGREDIENTS

225g (7½oz) icing sugar
30g (1oz) cocoa powder
125g (4oz) ground almonds
4 egg whites
30g (1oz) caster sugar

1 Sift the icing sugar and cocoa powder together. Sift the ground almonds over the top. Whisk the egg whites to soft peaks. Add the caster sugar and whisk until stiff. Gently fold in the icing sugar mixture, using a large metal spoon.

2 Fill a piping bag, fitted with a 1cm (½in) nozzle, with the mixture. Pipe small rounds about 2.5cm (1in) in diameter, spaced 2.5cm (1in) apart, on to the prepared baking sheets. Leave at room temperature for 15 minutes.

3 Bake in the preheated oven for 10–12 minutes. Leave the oven door slightly ajar to allow steam to escape. Remove the macaroons from the oven and leave for a few minutes before lifting them off the paper.

Oven temperature
180°C/350°F/gas 4

Baking time
10–12 minutes

Baking tins
Two flat baking sheets, lined with silicone paper

Makes
36

Storage
Keep for 3–4 days in an airtight container

Chocolate Walnut Biscuits

These wafer-thin buttery biscuits are a family favourite. They are also good made with other nuts such as hazelnuts or pecan nuts.

INGREDIENTS

200g (7oz) plain flour

⅛ tsp salt

30g (1oz) cocoa powder

½ tsp bicarbonate of soda

150g (5oz) unsalted butter

150g (5oz) dark brown sugar

30g (1oz) granulated sugar

1 egg yolk

1 tsp vanilla extract

90g (3oz) walnuts, very finely chopped

1 Sift the flour, salt, cocoa powder and soda together.

2 Beat the butter until soft, add both sugars and continue to beat until well blended. Stir in the egg yolk and vanilla. Fold in the flour mixture and the walnuts. With lightly floured hands, roll the dough into a sausage shape 5cm (2in) in diameter.

3 Wrap the dough in clingfilm and chill for at least 2 hours or freeze until the dough is very firm, about 1 hour.

4 Using a very thin, sharp knife, cut the dough into 2.5mm (⅛in) slices. Put them on the prepared baking sheets and bake in batches in the preheated oven for 8–10 minutes. Be careful not to let them burn or overcook.

5 Lift them off the paper and place on a flat surface to cool and crisp.

Oven temperature
190°C/375°F/gas 5

Baking time
8–10 minutes per batch

Baking tins
Two or three flat baking sheets, lined with silicone paper

Makes
28

Storage
Keep for 1 week in an airtight container

Freezing
Dough freezes for 1–2 months

Chocolate Almond Biscotti

In northern Italy these firm, dry biscuits are served accompanied by a glass of Vin Santo. The biscotti are dipped into the sweet wine to soften and to soak up the wine's rich taste.

INGREDIENTS

125g (4oz) almonds

300g (10oz) plain flour

1 tsp baking powder

½ tsp salt

180g (6oz) caster sugar

zest of ½ orange, very finely chopped

2 eggs

2 egg yolks

90g (3oz) plain chocolate, chopped into pea-size pieces (see page 32)

1 egg white, lightly beaten

1 Toast the almonds lightly on an ungreased baking sheet in the preheated oven for about 10 minutes. When they have cooled, chop half of them coarsely and set aside.

2 Finely grind the remaining almonds in a processor or blender. Sift the flour, baking powder and salt into a bowl. Stir in the sugar, ground nuts, and orange zest. Make a well in the centre of the dry ingredients and add the whole eggs and yolks. Stir from the centre, incorporating the flour, little by little, until the mixture starts to stick together. Add the chopped nuts and the chocolate pieces.

3 Turn out on to a floured surface, and, handling the dough as lightly as possible, divide it into 4 equal parts. Form each into a sausage shape approx. 23 x 4cm (9 x 1½in) and brush with the egg white. Place them, spaced apart, on the greased baking sheet. Bake in the preheated oven for 20 minutes. Remove from the oven. Reduce the oven temperature to the lower setting.

4 Cut the dough into 1cm (½in) slices on the diagonal. Lay the slices on the ungreased baking sheets.

5 Bake, turning once, for 25–30 minutes. Remove from the oven and leave on the baking sheet to cool completely.

Oven temperature
190°C/375°F/gas 5; then 140°C/275°F/ gas 1

Baking time
20 minutes first baking; 25–30 minutes second baking

Baking tins
Flat baking sheet, greased and floured; one or two flat baking sheets, ungreased

Makes
40

Storage
Keep for 2–3 weeks in an airtight container

Pies & Tarts

Fill a crisp pastry shell or crunchy biscuit crust with sumptuous chocolate to create a perfect dessert combination. There are so many delectable choices, from a Chocolate Pear Tart in which the fruit enhances the taste of the chocolate, to a light-as-air Chocolate Chiffon Pie topped with swirls of whipped cream, and a chocolate-rich version of Banoffee Pie. Ice cream and whipped cream, the classic accompaniments for dessert pies, are particularly apt when served with chocolate, for they intensify its unique flavour.

Mississippi Mud Pie

A favourite recipe in American Southern States cooking, this pie has a luscious chocolate filling, with a dash of coffee flavouring, enclosed in a light egg pastry shell.

INGREDIENTS

For the pastry shell

1 quantity Chocolate Pecan Pie pastry (see page 96)

For the filling

150g (5oz) butter

30g (1oz) plain chocolate, chopped (see page 32)

6 tbsp cocoa powder, sifted

2 tsp instant espresso coffee powder

3 eggs

250g (8oz) caster sugar

2 tbsp soured cream

3 tbsp golden syrup

1 tsp vanilla extract

white, milk and plain chocolate curls, to decorate (see page 43)

1 Allow the pastry to come to room temperature. Knead it briefly then roll it out on a lightly floured surface. Use the pastry to line the prepared tin, rolling it out a little thinner than for the Chocolate Pecan Pie. Chill the pastry shell while preparing the filling.

2 Put a baking sheet in the lower third of the oven and preheat the oven.

3 For the filling, gently melt the butter in a small saucepan. Remove from the heat and stir in the chocolate, cocoa powder and coffee, stirring until the chocolate has melted. Set aside.

4 Beat the eggs and sugar together until the mixture is creamy and blended, then add the soured cream, golden syrup and vanilla extract. Stir in the chocolate and butter mixture.

5 Pour the filling into the pastry shell. Bake on the hot baking sheet in the preheated oven for 35–40 minutes, or until the filling puffs up and forms a crust. Remove the pie to a wire rack to cool. The filling will sink a little and may crack slightly as it cools.

6 Before serving, decorate the pie with chocolate curls: a mixture of different coloured curls looks impressive. Vanilla ice cream is an excellent accompaniment for this pie.

Oven temperature
180°C/350°F/gas 4

Baking time
35–40 minutes

Baking tin
3.5cm (1½in) deep, 23cm (9in) diameter, loose-based flan tin, greased

Makes
8–10 slices

Storage
Keeps for 2 days in the refrigerator

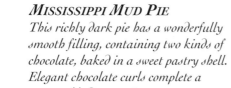

MISSISSIPPI MUD PIE
This richly dark pie has a wonderfully smooth filling, containing two kinds of chocolate, baked in a sweet pastry shell. Elegant chocolate curls complete a memorable dessert pie.

Large chocolate curls make a stylish topping

The sweet, creamy filling gives this pie its name

Chocolate Mousse Pie

This pie's shell is given texture and flavour by the addition of finely ground hazelnuts. The baked filling, based on eggs, cream and chocolate, has a luxury touch in brandy or rum, added just before baking.

DECORATING THE PIE
The top of the Chocolate Mousse Pie cracks as it cools. Large chocolate curls and a dusting of cocoa powder help cover the cracks and also integrate them into an eye-appealing decoration.

INGREDIENTS

For the pastry shell

60g (2oz) toasted and skinned hazelnuts (see page 38), finely ground

165g (5½oz) plain flour, sifted

30g (1oz) caster sugar

125g (4oz) lightly salted butter, diced

1 small egg, lightly beaten

a little iced water

For the filling

125g (4oz) plain or semi-sweet chocolate

60g (2oz) butter

2 eggs

100g (3½oz) caster sugar

2 tbsp flour

4 tbsp double cream

1½ tbsp rum or brandy

For the decoration

plain chocolate curls (see page 43)

cocoa powder

1 For the pastry, put the ground hazelnuts, flour and sugar in a large bowl. Add the butter and rub in with the fingertips until the mixture resembles fine breadcrumbs. Mix in sufficient egg and, if necessary, water, to make a stiff dough (the mixture should stick together in small clumps).

2 Turn the dough on to a lightly floured surface and form into a ball. Wrap in clingfilm and chill in the refrigerator for 30 minutes.

3 Preheat the oven to the higher temperature, putting a baking sheet in the lower third of the oven. Roll out the dough on a lightly floured surface and use to line the flan tin. Prick the base with a fork. Line the pastry with greaseproof paper weighed down with dried beans (to 'blind bake' the shell).

4 Put the tin on the hot baking sheet and bake for 10 minutes. Remove the paper and beans and bake for another 5–8 minutes. Cool on a wire rack. Reduce the oven temperature to the lower setting.

5 For the filling, melt the chocolate and butter together (see page 34). Set aside to cool. Whisk the eggs and sugar in a large heatproof bowl set over hot water for about 10 minutes, or until the mixture forms a ribbon when the whisk is lifted. Sift the flour over the top and fold it in. Fold in the chocolate, cream and alcohol.

6 Pour the filling into the pastry shell and bake on the hot baking sheet for 15 minutes. Remove to a wire rack to cool.

7 To decorate, arrange the chocolate curls on top of the pie and sift a dusting of cocoa over them.

Oven temperature
200°C/400°F/gas 6
then
190°C/375°F/gas 5

Baking time
15–18 minutes for the pastry shell; 15 minutes for the pie

Baking tin
3.5cm (1½ in) deep, 23cm (9in) diameter, loose-based flan tin, greased

Makes
8 slices

Storage
Keeps for 2 days in the refrigerator, but best eaten when baked

Chocolate Chiffon Pie

Stiffly beaten egg whites give an airy lightness to the deliciously creamy, richly flavoured chocolate custard for this pie's filling.

INGREDIENTS

For the biscuit crust

150g (5oz) digestive biscuits, crushed

100g (3½oz) ground hazelnuts, walnuts or almonds

90g (3oz) unsalted butter, melted

For the filling

2 tsp gelatine

2 tbsp cold water

2 eggs, separated

150g (5oz) caster sugar

250ml (8fl oz) milk

200g (7oz) plain chocolate, chopped into small pieces (see page 32)

2 tsp vanilla extract

300ml (½ pint) double cream

pinch of salt

For the decoration

150ml (¼ pint) double cream, whipped

plain chocolate curls (see page 43)

1 Put the biscuit crumbs and nuts in a bowl, pour in the butter and mix together lightly with a fork. Turn into the flan tin, pressing the mixture in an even layer over the sides and bottom to make a biscuit crust.

2 Bake the biscuit crust in the preheated oven for 10 minutes. Cool on a wire rack. Chill in the tin until needed.

3 For the filling, put the gelatine and water in a cup and leave until the gelatine is spongy, about 5 minutes. Set the cup in hot water until the gelatine has dissolved.

4 Whisk the egg yolks with 90g (3oz) of the sugar. Bring the milk to the boil, pour it over the egg yolks, whisking constantly, then return the mixture to the saucepan. Stir with a wooden spoon over low heat until the mixture thickens enough to coat the spoon. Do not allow it to boil or it will curdle. Remove the custard from the heat and stir in the gelatine. Add the chocolate pieces and vanilla and stir until blended. Set aside to cool.

5 Lightly whip the cream. Fold it into the cooled chocolate mixture with a large metal spoon. Whisk the egg whites with the salt until stiff, add the remaining sugar and whisk until the egg whites form stiff peaks. Carefully fold the egg whites into the mixture, ensuring that the chiffon is thoroughly blended without overmixing. Pour into the prepared crust, smoothing the top with a palette knife, if liked. Chill the pie for at least 2 hours or until set, keeping it in the refrigerator until needed.

Oven temperature
180°C/350°F/gas 4

Baking time
10 minutes

Baking tin
3.5cm (1½in) deep, 23cm (9in) diameter, loose-based flan tin

Makes
8 slices

Storage
Keeps for 2 days in the refrigerator

* Warning
This recipe contains uncooked egg whites (see page 9)

DECORATING THE PIE
Rosettes of firmly whipped cream (see page 48) are piped round the top edge of the Chocolate Chiffon Pie. Small chocolate curls, set on top of the cream rosettes, provide a final neat touch of chocolate.

Chocolate Pecan Pie

This is a variation of the American favourite, Pecan Pie. The dark chocolate filling is rum-flavoured.

INGREDIENTS

For the pastry shell

190g (6½oz) plain flour, sifted
2 tbsp caster sugar
½ tsp salt
100g (3½oz) chilled unsalted butter, cut into small pieces
1 egg yolk
2 tbsp iced water

For the filling

60g (2oz) butter
2 tbsp cocoa powder
250ml (8fl oz) golden syrup
3 eggs
90g (3oz) soft dark brown sugar
2 tbsp rum
250g (8oz) pecan nuts

1 To make the pastry, sift the flour, sugar and salt into a bowl. Rub the butter into the flour with your fingertips until the mixture resembles oatmeal. Blend the egg yolk with the water and fork it lightly into the mixture until it sticks together in small clumps.

2 Form the dough into a ball, wrap in clingfilm and chill for 30 minutes. Roll out the pastry and line the flan tin. Chill while making the filling.

3 Put a baking sheet in the oven while it is preheating. For the filling, gently melt the butter, then, off the heat, stir in the cocoa and golden syrup. Lightly beat the eggs with the sugar and rum. Stir in the syrup mixture. Chop half the nuts and add to the mixture. Pour into the pastry shell. Arrange the remaining nuts over the top.

4 Bake the pie on the hot baking sheet in the preheated oven for 35–40 minutes, or until the filling is just set. Cover the pie with foil if the pastry becomes too dark. Serve the pie warm or at room temperature.

 Oven temperature
180°C/350°F/gas 4

Baking time
35–40 minutes

Baking tin
24cm (9½ in) loose-based flan tin, greased

Makes
8–10 slices

Storage
Keeps for 2 days in an air-tight container in the refrigerator

Chocolate Fruit Tartlets

These delicious tartlets are filled with cream and fresh fruits. The chocolate pastry base is easy to make; the ingredients are mixed in a saucepan.

INGREDIENTS

For the pastry

150g (5oz) lightly salted butter, cut into small pieces
60g (2oz) soft dark brown sugar
3 tbsp cocoa powder
250g (8oz) plain flour
1 small egg white

For the filling and decoration

150g (5oz) redcurrant jelly
1 tbsp water
150ml (¼ pint) double cream, lightly whipped
750g (1½lb) fresh berry fruit
chocolate leaves (see page 43)

1 For the pastry, stir the butter, sugar and cocoa together in a saucepan over a low heat until the butter has melted and the ingredients are blended. Take the saucepan off the heat and stir in the flour, then enough egg white to make a firm dough. Wrap in clingfilm and chill for 15 minutes.

2 Divide the chilled dough into eight balls. Roll each one out between sheets of clingfilm. Using a 10cm (4in) plain biscuit cutter, cut each piece of pastry into a round.

3 Line the tartlet tins with the rounds, prick the bases with a fork and chill for 15 minutes.

4 Bake the pastry shells in the preheated oven for 20–25 minutes. Remove from the oven and cool on a wire rack before carefully taking the pastry shells from the tins.

Oven temperature
180°C/350°F/gas 4

Baking time
20–25 minutes

Baking tin
Eight 6cm (2½in) tartlet tins

Makes
8

Storage
Unfilled pastry shells keep for 3 days, tightly wrapped

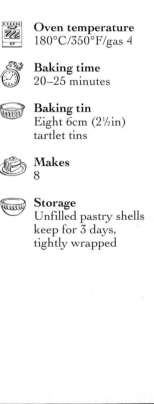

TO FINISH THE FRUIT TARTLETS

Make a redcurrant glaze by gently melting the redcurrant jelly with the water. Brush a thin layer of the glaze over the inside of the pastry shells. Whip the cream until it forms soft peaks and spoon it into the pastry shells. Spoon the fruits on top of the cream and brush them with redcurrant glaze. Set chocolate leaves among them.

Redcurrant glaze gives the fruit a glistening finish

Plain chocolate leaves contrast well with the fruit

Chocolate Pear Tart

Pears and chocolate go together very well – which explains why there are so many desserts based on the combination. This recipe puts the two together in a delicious almond pastry shell. Choose a firm, ripe dessert pear, such as Comice or Williams.

INGREDIENTS

For the pastry shell

165g (5½oz) plain flour	
30g (1oz) caster sugar	
30g (1oz) ground almonds	
½ tsp salt	
125g (4oz) chilled unsalted butter, diced	
3–4 tablespoons iced water	

For the filling

4 or 5 ripe dessert pears, depending on size	
1½ tbsp caster sugar	
90g (3oz) unsalted butter	
45g (1½oz) cocoa powder	
1 egg	
180g (6oz) granulated sugar	
45g (1½oz) plain flour	
1 tsp vanilla extract	
icing sugar, to decorate	

1 For the pastry, sift the flour, sugar, ground almonds and salt into a bowl. Add the butter and rub it into the flour with your fingertips until the mixture resembles fine breadcrumbs. Using a fork, mix in just enough water for the mixture to cling together in small clumps.

2 Turn the dough out on to a flat surface and quickly form it into a ball. Wrap in clingfilm and chill for at least 30 minutes.

3 Roll the pastry out on a lightly floured surface and line the prepared tin with it. Put it in the freezer while you prepare the pears.

4 Peel, quarter and core the pears. Prick the pastry with a fork and sprinkle with the caster sugar. Arrange the pears on the uncooked pastry, put into the preheated oven and bake for 15 minutes. Remove from the oven and set on a wire rack until ready to fill.

5 Meanwhile, complete the filling. Melt the butter, add the cocoa and stir until smooth. Whisk the egg with the sugar, then add the cocoa mixture. Sift the flour over the top of the mixture and fold in. Stir in the vanilla extract. Pour the filling over the top of the pears and smooth into as even a layer as possible with a spatula.

6 Put the tart back in the oven for 15 minutes, or until the filling has set. Remove to a wire rack to cool. Before serving, decorate the top of the pie with a light sprinkling of icing sugar.

Oven temperature
200°C/400°F/gas 6

Baking time
15 minutes for the base and pears; 15–20 minutes with chocolate filling

Baking tin
23cm (9in) loose-based flan tin, greased

Makes
8–10 slices

Storage
Keeps for 2 days in the refrigerator

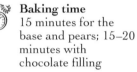

Chocolate Banoffee Pie

This dessert gets its name from its extravagant layering of ingredients: a blend of chocolate and cream on a biscuit base, then a layer of smooth toffee, topped with slices of banana and, finally, thickly whipped cream piled high with chocolate curls.

INGREDIENTS

For the filling

Two 400ml (14fl oz) cans sweetened condensed milk

150g (5oz) continental plain or bittersweet chocolate, melted (see page 33)

125ml (4fl oz) double cream

1 tsp vanilla extract

For the biscuit crust

260g (8½oz) digestive biscuits, crushed

90g (3oz) lightly salted butter, melted

For the topping

3 small ripe bananas

300ml (½ pint) double cream, whipped

plain, milk and white chocolate curls (see page 43)

cocoa powder for dusting

1 Puncture a small hole in the top of each condensed milk can. Set them in a saucepan large enough to immerse them in water. Bring to the boil and simmer for two hours, with the pan partially covered, adding more water as necessary. Remove the cans and cool.

2 For the biscuit crust, put the biscuits in a bowl and pour over the butter. Mix together and turn into the prepared tin, pressing them down in an even layer, first over the sides and then on the bottom to make the crust. Bake in the preheated oven for 10 minutes. Cool on a wire rack then chill until needed.

3 Continue making the filling. Cool the chocolate to tepid. Whisk the cream until it is just thick and fold it into the chocolate. Fold in the vanilla. Spoon the mixture into the biscuit crust, spreading it evenly. Chill until set.

4 Open the tins of cooled condensed milk, which will have cooked into a toffee-like cream. Pour into a bowl and whisk until smooth. Spoon over the chocolate layer in the crust and chill until ready to serve.

5 Complete the topping before serving. Slice the bananas and arrange them over the toffee layer. Spoon the cream on top. Pile on the chocolate curls and finish with a light dusting of cocoa powder.

Oven temperature
180°C/350°F/gas 4

Baking time
10 minutes

Baking tin
3.5cm (1½in) deep, 23cm (9in) diameter, loose-based flan tin, greased

Makes
10–12 slices

Storage
Keeps for 2 days in the refrigerator, without banana and cream topping

Step ahead
Make toffee cream 1 day ahead, and keep in refrigerator

Hot Chocolate Puddings

What could be better to take the chill out of a cold winter's day than a hot chocolate dessert? The aroma of chocolate wafting through the air arouses the taste buds to the joy of what's to come. There are a number of delightful winter warmers to tempt the palate, from a light, airy soufflé to a sumptuous, orange-scented, steamed pudding. For a special occasion, you might consider elegant, thin crêpes filled with luscious chocolate cream, or an aromatic rum-flavoured chocolate fondue. All warming desserts for a winter treat.

Chocolate Rum Fondue

A very satisfying dessert for chocoholics. Place the warm chocolate fondue in the centre of the table with a large platter of cake, biscuits, freshly prepared fruit and forks for dipping. The fondue can be flavoured with any liqueur or spirit or left plain.

Serve an eye-catching display of fruits, cakes and biscuits for dipping into the fondue

INGREDIENTS

125g (4oz) caster sugar

125ml (4fl oz) water

180g (6oz) continental plain chocolate

60g (2oz) butter

50ml (2fl oz) rum

pound, angelfood or plain cake cut into 2.5cm (1in) cubes

sponge fingers or other plain biscuits

fresh whole strawberries, small wedges of fresh pineapple or pear, cape gooseberries, orange segments, cherries and other fresh fruit

1 Put the sugar and water in a saucepan and stir over gentle heat until the sugar has dissolved. Remove from the heat and set aside to cool.

2 Melt the chocolate with the butter (see page 34). Stir the chocolate into the sugar syrup.

3 To serve, reheat the fondue in a microwave or in the top of a double boiler set over hot water. Stir the rum into the chocolate. Pour into a fondue or chafing dish. Serve the fondue warm, with a selection of fruits, biscuits and cubes of cake.

NOTE: The chocolate may have to be gently reheated half-way through. If you use a fondue or chafing dish with spirit flame, do not keep it on all the time as the chocolate can overheat and become grainy.

Makes
6–8 servings

Storage
The fondue keeps 2 days in the refrigerator

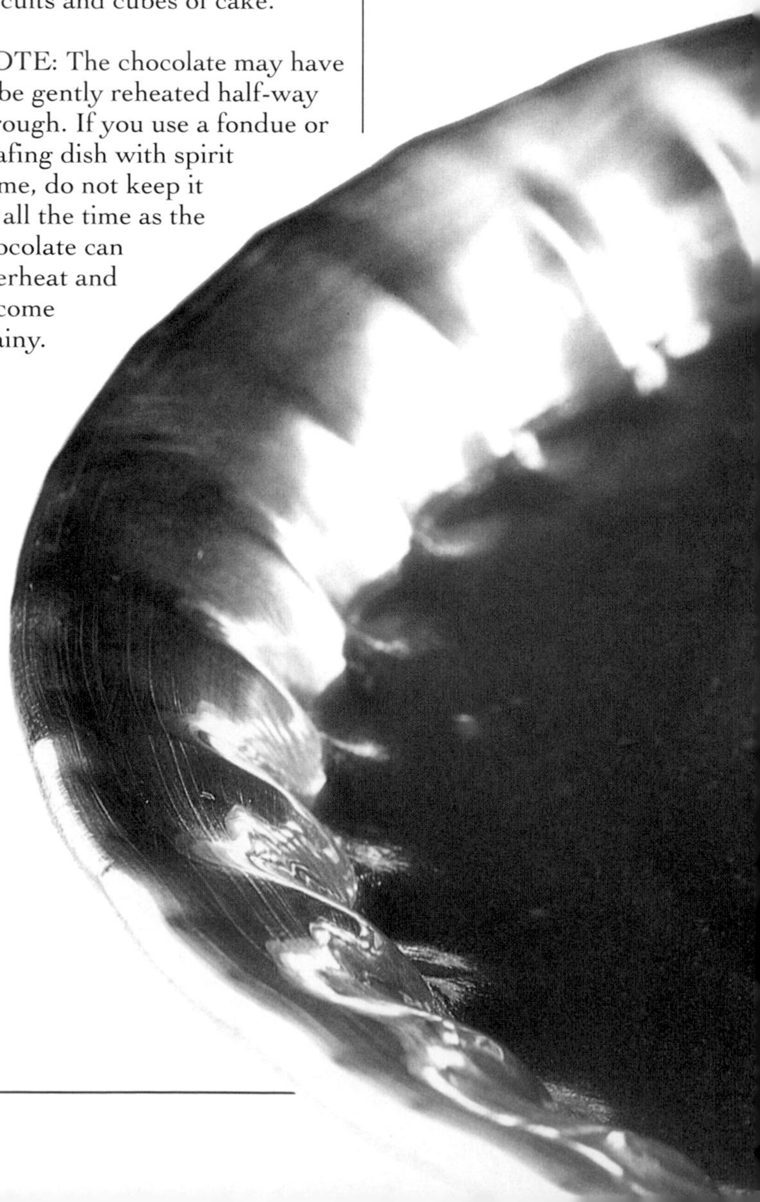

pineapple piece

apple slice

melon ball

CHOCOLATE RUM FONDUE
Prepare bite-size pieces of fruit and cake for serving with the fondue.

plain cake

kiwi fruit

Firm pieces of fresh fruit will not slip off the fondue fork

Chocolate Bread Pudding

Bread and Butter Pudding becomes much more than a nursery dish when a creamy chocolate custard is added to it.

INGREDIENTS

250ml (8fl oz) double cream
250ml (8fl oz) milk
¼ tsp salt
25g (¾oz) cocoa powder
3 eggs
125g (4oz) granulated sugar
1 tsp vanilla extract
3 soft bread rolls or baps
30g (1oz) unsalted butter, softened

1 Bring the cream, milk and salt slowly to the boil in a heavy-based saucepan, then remove from the heat. Sift the cocoa powder over the top and whisk until well blended. Beat the eggs and sugar together then beat in the cocoa mixture. Add the vanilla extract.

2 Cut the rolls into thin slices and butter them. Place enough slices in the dish so that the top layer comes above the rim of the dish. Pour the custard in round the sides. The pudding can be prepared up to this stage an hour or two before baking, if preferred.

3 Put the dish in a roasting pan. Fill the pan with hot water to come half-way up the sides of the dish.

4 Bake in the preheated oven for 40 minutes, or until set. If the top crusts are not crisp and brown, crisp the edges under a hot grill. Serve the pudding with a jug of thick cream, if liked.

Oven temperature
160°C/325°F/gas 3

Baking time
40 minutes

Baking dish
1 litre (1¾ pint) soufflé dish, greased with butter

Makes
6 servings

Step ahead
Make the pudding an hour or two before baking

Chocolate Soufflé

This is a superbly light and very chocolatey soufflé with a hint of alcohol to give it a touch of extravagance.

INGREDIENTS

100g (3½oz) plain chocolate
3 tbsp cornflour
250ml (8fl oz) milk
60g (2oz) caster sugar
3 tbsp Grand Marnier, Cointreau or Curaçao
30g (1oz) unsalted butter
5 egg whites
a pinch of salt
3 egg yolks
To serve
Crème Anglaise (see page 134) or
175ml (6fl oz) thick cream, whipped

1 Break the chocolate into pieces and melt it (see page 33). Set aside.

2 Mix the cornflour to a smooth paste with a few tablespoons of the milk and then gradually stir in the rest of the milk. Pour into a saucepan, add half the sugar and bring to the boil, stirring constantly. Boil for 1 minute, remove from the heat and stir in the chocolate

and the liqueur. Dot the surface with the butter and set aside until tepid.

3 Meanwhile, whisk the egg whites with the salt until they form soft peaks. Add the remaining sugar and continue whisking until the mixture is glossy and stiff.

4 Stir the egg yolks, one at a time, into the chocolate mixture, then fold in a large spoonful of the stiffly beaten whites. Carefully fold in the rest of the whites, using a large metal spoon.

5 Pour the mixture into the prepared soufflé dish and bake in the centre of the preheated oven for 35 minutes, or until the soufflé has risen, the top is brown and the centre still quivers.

6 Serve the soufflé at once, with the Crème Anglaise served separately. Alternatively, serve with whipped cream.

Oven temperature
190°C/375°F/gas 5

Baking time
35 minutes

Baking dish
1 litre (1¾ pint) soufflé dish, buttered and lightly sprinkled with caster sugar, and with 10cm (4in) wide silicone paper collar, also buttered and sprinkled with caster sugar, tied round

Makes
4 servings

Chocolate Amaretti-filled Crêpes

Simple crêpes become something special when given a filling full of contrasts: the taste of chocolate mingles with that of almonds; crushed biscuits add crunch to the smooth mixture of chocolate and cream. You could omit flaming the pancakes with brandy, if preferred.

INGREDIENTS

For the crêpes

125g (4oz) plain flour
¼ tsp salt
3 eggs
250ml (8fl oz) milk
2 tbsp unsalted butter, melted
oil or butter for greasing

For the filling

275ml (9fl oz) milk
3 egg yolks
75g (2½oz) caster sugar
30g (1oz) plain flour
75g (2½oz) plain chocolate, chopped (see page 32)
1 tbsp almond liqueur, such as Amaretto di Saronno
150ml (¼ pint) whipping cream, lightly whipped
60g (2oz) amaretti biscuits, crushed
melted butter, for brushing
sugar, for sprinkling
3–4 tbsp brandy, for flaming

1 For the crêpes, sift the flour and salt into a bowl, make a well in the centre and add the eggs and milk. Whisk from the centre, slowly blending the ingredients, then add the melted butter. Be careful not to overmix. Let the batter stand for at least 20 minutes. It should have the consistency of thin cream. Thin the mixture with a few tablespoons of water, if necessary.

2 Brush a 23cm (9in) crêpe pan or frying pan with oil. Heat the pan until very hot (a drop of batter will sizzle at once). Add a serving spoon of batter to the pan, tilting it quickly so the bottom is evenly coated. (Pour out any excess batter and adjust the amount for the next crêpe.) Cook over high heat until browned, then turn the crêpe over and cook for 10 seconds on the second side. It may take a few crêpes before the consistency, amount of batter and heat are just right. Stack the pancakes on a plate once they are cooked.

3 For the filling, bring the milk to the boil. Whisk the egg yolks, sugar and flour together in a medium-size bowl. Whisk in the hot milk, then return the mixture to the saucepan and simmer for 2 minutes, stirring constantly. Remove from the heat and stir in the chocolate and liqueur. When the chocolate cream is cool, fold in the lightly whipped cream and the amaretti crumbs.

4 Grease a large flameproof gratin dish with butter. Place a spoonful of the filling on the underside of a crêpe, roll it up and place it seam-side down in the dish. Alternatively, fold the crêpes into quarters and overlap them in the dish. Continue until all the crêpes have been used.

5 Brush the tops with melted butter and sprinkle over some sugar. Cover with a piece of silicone paper. Bake in the preheated oven for 15–20 minutes, or until hot. Heat the brandy in a small pan, flame it, and pour over the crêpes. Serve immediately.

Oven temperature
180°C/350°F/gas 4

Baking time
15–20 minutes

Baking dish
1 litre (1¾ pint) gratin dish

Makes
About 18 crêpes

Storage
Unfilled crêpes keep for 2 days in the refrigerator; filling keeps for 2 days in the refrigerator

Freezing
Unfilled crêpes keep for 2 months, with a layer of clingfilm or silicone paper between each crêpe

Chocolate Orange Puddings

These individual puddings are baked in the oven, in a bain-marie, which helps give them the texture of a light steamed pudding.

INGREDIENTS

finely grated zest of ½ orange

100g (3½oz) plain chocolate, melted (see page 33)

6 eggs, separated

60g (2oz) granulated sugar

100g (3½oz) ground almonds

60g (2oz) chocolate cake crumbs

pinch of salt

For the sauce

300ml (½ pint) double cream

2–3 tbsp caster sugar

1–2 tbsp Cointreau or other orange-flavoured liqueur

1 Mix the orange zest into the chocolate. Whisk the egg yolks with the sugar until pale. Fold in the chocolate then the almonds and the cake crumbs.

2 Whisk the egg whites with the salt until stiff. Fold a large spoonful of the egg whites into the chocolate mixture to lighten it, then carefully fold in the remaining whites.

3 Pour the batter into the prepared moulds and cover the moulds with buttered foil. Put the moulds in a roasting pan at least 5cm (2in) deep. Pour in enough hot water to come half way up the sides of the moulds.

4 Carefully put the roasting pan into the preheated oven and bake for 30 minutes, or until set.

5 To make the sauce, whip the cream until it starts to thicken slightly. Add 2 tablespoons of the sugar and 1 tablespoon of the liqueur. Taste and adjust the flavour as desired.

6 To unmould the puddings, slip a knife around the edge of the moulds; put a serving plate on top of each mould, reverse, and give a sharp tap to the top of the mould to help release the pudding. Spoon sauce over the puddings and serve hot.

Oven temperature
180°C/350°F/gas 4

Baking time
30 minutes

Baking dishes
Eight 175ml/6fl oz metal pudding moulds, buttered and sugared

Makes
8

Storage
The puddings are best served at once

Chocolate Steamed Pudding

Cake crumbs instead of the more traditional flour produce a light and airy steamed pudding, unlike any remembered from past school-days. The pudding can be flavoured with a favourite liqueur, or with ginger as in the variation given opposite.

INGREDIENTS

180g (6oz) chocolate cake

2 tsp ground cinnamon

90g (3oz) continental plain chocolate

175ml (6fl oz) milk

60g (2oz) butter

60g (2oz) granulated sugar

3 eggs, separated

1 tsp vanilla extract

small pinch of cream of tartar

To serve

Bitter Chocolate Sauce (see page 134) or 175ml (6fl oz) whipping cream, whipped

1 Break the chocolate cake into pieces. Put the pieces in a food processor or blender and pulse the machine briefly to make crumbs. Stir the cinnamon into the crumbs.

2 Melt the chocolate with the milk (see page 34), stir until smooth and set aside.

3 Cream the butter with the sugar. Add the egg yolks, one at a time, and stir until blended. Add the chocolate milk to the cake crumbs and mix together. Turn the chocolate crumb mixture into the creamed butter and blend together. Add the vanilla.

4 Whisk the egg whites and cream of tartar until they form stiff peaks. Fold into the chocolate mixture. Turn into the buttered bowl. Cover the bowl with a pleated piece of silicone paper. Lay a tea towel over the top and tie securely under the edge of the bowl with string.

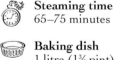

Steaming time
65–75 minutes

Baking dish
1 litre (1¾ pint) pudding basin, thickly buttered

Makes
6–8 servings

Bring up the ends of the cloth and tie together to make a handle. Trim off any excess silicone paper.

5 Put a trivet or upside down saucer in the bottom of a deep saucepan. Fill the pan with enough water to come half-way up the bowl. Heat the water and when it is simmering lower the pudding into the pan, cover, and steam for 65–75 minutes.

6 Carefully lift the pudding out of the water. Remove the cloth and paper. Slip a knife around the inside edge of the bowl to loosen the pudding and turn it out on to a deep serving dish.

7 Pour warm Bitter Chocolate Sauce over the pudding before serving it, with any remaining sauce served separately in a jug. Alternatively, serve the pudding with whipped cream.

CHOCOLATE STEAMED PUDDING

This is a deliciously rich yet light hot pudding. For a more spicy treat, try the ginger-flavoured alternative below.

VARIATION

Ginger Chocolate Steamed Pudding
Omit the cinnamon and vanilla extract and add 1 teaspoon ground ginger, 2 tablespoons of chopped stem ginger and 1 tablespoon of the stem ginger syrup.

Cold Desserts

A refreshing lightness characterizes these cool desserts, which include mousses, elegant terrines and smooth creams. A fine array of chocolates are mixed with memorable combinations of flavourings – white chocolate with limes or plain chocolate with rum or an orange liqueur, for example, providing both unusual and classical partnerships. In several recipes, coffee emphasizes the richness of the chocolate. Sauces and creams, and many suggestions for elegant decorations, put the perfect finishing touch to every dessert.

Chocolate Velvet Mousse

INGREDIENTS

150g (5oz) continental plain chocolate, melted

3 eggs, separated

75g (2½oz) unsalted butter, cut into small pieces

1 tbsp crème de cacao or Tia Maria or 2 tsp vanilla extract

1 egg white

pinch of salt

1 quantity Crème Anglaise (see page 134)

melted plain chocolate (see page 33), to decorate

This is a gloriously smooth mousse – hence its evocative name. It is elegant served simply with a light Crème Anglaise, but also makes an excellent base for more adventurous desserts.

1 Melt the chocolate (see page 33). While still hot, beat in the egg yolks, one at a time. Stir in the butter and when the mixture is smooth, add the liqueur or vanilla extract.

2 Whisk all 4 egg whites with a pinch of salt until the whites form stiff peaks. Fold a heaped spoonful of the whites into the chocolate mixture to lighten it, then carefully fold in the remaining whites.

3 Turn the mixture into the dish, cover and chill until it is set – about 4 hours.

4 To serve, pour Crème Anglaise on to individual dessert plates. Warm a serving spoon in hot water and then dip the spoon into the mousse to make an oval-shaped scoop. Put scoops, round-side up, on the Crème Anglaise. To decorate, pipe lines of melted chocolate on top, using a cocktail stick to 'pull' it into a pattern.

Equipment
20cm (8in) gratin or other shallow dish

Serves
6

Storage
Keeps for 1 week, covered, in the refrigerator

* Warning
This recipe contains uncooked egg whites (see page 9)

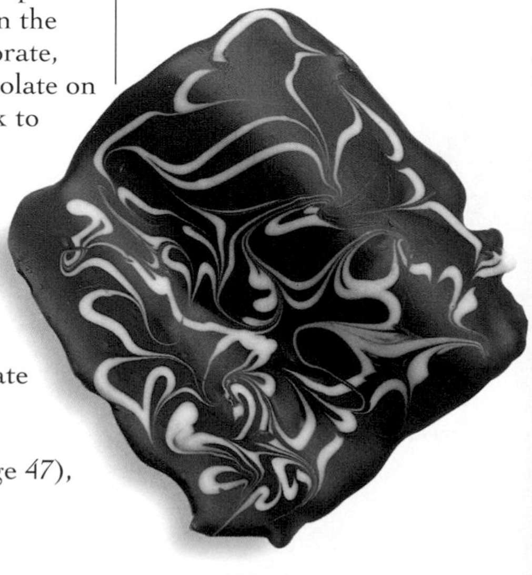

Marbled Millefeuilles
(See below, left.)

VARIATION
Marbled Millefeuilles
Put spoonfuls of Chocolate Velvet Mousse between marbled plain and white chocolate waves (see page 47), stacking them up as you would a layer cake.

MARBLED MILLEFEUILLE *sets creamy Chocolate Velvet Mousse between crisp waves of plain and white chocolate.*

Chocolate waves are shaped over wooden-spoon handles

Chocolate Velvet Mousse spooned between chocolate waves 7cm (3in) square

White Chocolate and Lime Mousse

In this deliciously simple mousse, the soft, creamy flavour of white chocolate contrasts with the marvellous tang of fresh limes – smoother and less tart than lemon.

INGREDIENTS

For the mousse

1½ tsp gelatine

2 tbsp cold water

250g (8oz) white chocolate, chopped (see page 32)

150ml (¼ pint) double cream

5 tbsp lime juice

grated rind of 1 lime

2 egg whites

pinch of salt

2 tsp caster sugar

lime zest, to decorate

1 Sprinkle the gelatine over the water in a cup and leave for 5 minutes to turn spongy. Put the cup in a bowl of hot water and leave for the gelatine to dissolve.

2 Carefully melt the chocolate (see page 33). Whip the cream until it forms soft peaks. Stir a large spoonful of cream into the chocolate. Add the gelatine, lime juice and rind, and fold in the remaining cream.

3 Whisk the egg whites with the salt until they form soft peaks. Add the sugar and whisk for 30 seconds more. Fold a large spoonful of egg whites into the chocolate then fold in the remaining whites.

4 Either leave the mixture in the bowl or spoon it into six ramekins and chill for 4–6 hours. To serve, leave the mousse in the ramekins or put spoonfuls from the large bowl into Chocolate Hazelnut Tuile baskets (see page 89). Decorate with twists of lime zest.

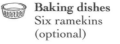

Baking dishes
Six ramekins (optional)

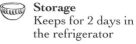

Makes
6 servings

Storage
Keeps for 2 days in the refrigerator

✳ **Warning**
This recipe contains uncooked egg whites (see page 9)

Chocolate Charlotte

The traditional charlotte is given a sophisticated touch here with the addition of chocolate and coffee.

INGREDIENTS

180g (6oz) continental plain chocolate

150g (5oz) unsalted butter, cut into small pieces

45g (1½oz) cocoa powder

2 eggs

90g (3oz) caster sugar

1–2 tbsp white rum

300ml (½ pint) double cream, whipped

small cup of strong black coffee

approx 325g (11oz) sponge fingers

1 Melt the chocolate (see page 33). While still warm, whisk in the butter, then the cocoa.

2 Whisk the eggs and sugar over a bowl of hot water until the mixture is very thick

and leaves a ribbon trail when the whisk is lifted. Using a metal spoon, carefully fold in the chocolate mixture, rum and whipped cream.

3 Brush coffee on the flat side of the sponge fingers and line the bottom and sides of the mould, cutting the fingers to shape where necessary, and placing the brushed side inwards. Spoon the chocolate mixture into the mould, cover with clingfilm and chill in the refrigerator overnight.

4 An hour before serving, turn the charlotte out on to a dessert plate and leave at room temperature.

Baking dish
17cm (6½in) diameter, 1.5 litre (2½ pints) capacity, charlotte mould, lined with clingfilm, leaving an overlap at the top edge

Makes
10 servings

Storage
Keeps for 3–4 days in the refrigerator

✳ **Warning**
This recipe contains lightly cooked eggs (see page 9)

Chocolate Amaretti Mousses

These delectable individual mousses need only the simplest decoration – like the crushed biscuits I have suggested here.

INGREDIENTS

150g (5oz) plain chocolate

2 tbsp rum or brandy

2 tbsp strong black coffee

1 tbsp cocoa powder

4 eggs, separated

150ml (¼ pint) double cream, whipped

60g (2oz) amaretti biscuits, crushed

1 Melt the chocolate, liqueur, coffee and cocoa powder together (see page 34). Stir until the mixture is smooth. While the mixture is still warm, whisk in the egg yolks, one at a time.

2 Whisk the egg whites, preferably in a copper bowl, until they are stiff. Fold a quarter of the whites into the chocolate to lighten the mixture, then fold in the remainder. Whip the cream until it holds soft peaks and fold into the chocolate mousse.

3 Put a heaped tablespoon of the crushed amaretti biscuits on a piece of clingfilm, seal, and set aside for decoration.

4 Put the remaining biscuit crumbs evenly in the bottom of the 8 ramekins and fill with the mousse. Chill in the refrigerator for 3–4 hours before serving, sprinkled with the reserved biscuit crumbs.

Baking dishes
Eight ramekins

Makes
8 servings

Storage
Keep for 2 days in the refrigerator

Freezing
2 months

* Warning
This recipe contains lightly cooked eggs (see page 9)

Iced Chocolate Soufflés

The plain exterior of these soufflés disguises a very rich dessert, for it contains two forms of chocolate, a generous splash of liqueur and plenty of whipped cream.

* Warning
This recipe contains lightly cooked egg whites (see page 9)

INGREDIENTS

30g (1oz) cocoa powder

60g (2oz) plain chocolate, chopped (see page 32)

125ml (4fl oz) water

100g (3½oz) caster sugar

2 egg whites

2 tbsp Grand Marnier or white rum

300ml (½ pint) double cream, whipped

chocolate curls, to decorate (see page 42)

1 Melt the cocoa, chocolate and 4 tablespoons of the water together (see page 34).

2 Dissolve the sugar and the remaining water in a small, heavy-based saucepan, bring to the boil and boil without stirring until the temperature reaches the soft ball stage (115°C/240°F on a sugar thermometer). While the sugar is boiling, whisk the egg whites until stiff.

3 Pour the hot sugar syrup in a steady stream over the whites, while continuing to whisk, and keep whisking until the mixture is thick and cool, about 10 minutes.

4 Fold the chocolate into the whites using a large metal spoon and then fold in the alcohol and the whipped cream. Spoon into the ramekins and freeze for at least 3 hours until the mousses are firm.

5 Before serving, remove the ramekins from the freezer and leave them in the refrigerator to soften for about 1½ hours. Peel away the paper collars and decorate the soufflés with chocolate curls.

Baking dishes
Four ramekins, each with a silicone paper collar extending 3.5cm (1½in) above the top of the ramekin

Makes
4 servings

Freezing
2 weeks, if completely wrapped

Chocolate Meringue Sandwiches

This excellent dinner party dessert is a clever combination of two recipes found in this book.

INGREDIENTS

For the meringues

1 quantity Chocolate Meringues (see page 81)

For the filling and decoration

1 quantity chocolate bavarois (see below)

150ml (¼ pint) double cream, whipped

60–90g (2–3oz) raspberries

chocolate curls (see page 43)

1 Spoon the Chocolate Meringue mixture into a nylon piping bag fitted with a 5mm (¼in) plain tube.

2 Fix the corners of the prepared silicone paper to the baking sheets with dabs of butter. Starting from the inside of the marked circles, pipe the mixture in coils.

3 Bake the meringues in the preheated oven for 1–1½ hours, or until crisp. Peel the meringues off the paper and put on a wire rack to cool.

4 Make the chocolate bavarois and pour it into the prepared tin. Chill until set.

5 Turn the bavarois out on to greaseproof paper. Peel away the silicone paper. Cut eight 7cm (3in) rounds from the bavarois. Sandwich the bavarois rounds with whipped cream between 2 meringues. Decorate with cream, raspberries and chocolate curls.

 Oven temperature
120°C/250°F/gas ½

Baking time
1–1½ hours

Baking tins
Two flat baking sheets lined with silicone paper, each marked with eight 7cm (3in) circles with 1cm (½in) spaces between; 28cm (11in) shallow baking tin, lined with silicone paper

Makes
8

Storage
Keep for 2 days in the refrigerator

Chocolate Bavarois Dessert

Chocolate-flavoured bavarois – a light mousse set with gelatine – is given the glamour treatment here, set in a case made from chocolate-striped sponge cake.

INGREDIENTS

For the sponge case

165g (5½oz) plain flour

15g (½oz) cocoa powder

6 eggs, separated

½ tsp vanilla extract

190g (6½oz) caster sugar

30g (1oz) icing sugar

2 tbsp orange marmalade, heated with 1 tbsp water

For the chocolate bavarois

¾ tbsp gelatine

4 tbsp fresh orange juice

175ml (6fl oz) milk

3 eggs, separated

90g (3oz) caster sugar

2 tbsp cocoa powder, sifted

60g (2oz) continental plain chocolate, chopped into small pieces (see page 32)

pinch of salt

90ml (3fl oz) double cream, lightly whipped

2 tbsp orange liqueur

For the decoration

white chocolate curls (see page 43)

strips of crystallized peel (see page 127)

1 For the sponge case, sift 75g (2½ oz) of flour with the cocoa on to greaseproof paper. Sift the remaining 90g (3oz) of flour on to a second piece.

2 Whisk the egg yolks, vanilla, and all but 2 tablespoons of the sugar together until the mixture is thick and forms a ribbon when the whisk is lifted.

3 Whisk the whites until they form soft peaks, add the remaining sugar, and beat for another minute until firm.

4 Fold a spoonful of whites into the yolk mixture to loosen it, then carefully fold in the remaining whites. Before the whites are completely blended scoop half of the mixture out into another bowl. Sift the flour and cocoa mixture over one bowl and fold in. Sift the flour over the other bowl and fold in.

5 Spoon the mixtures into 2 piping bags fitted with 1cm (½in) plain nozzles. Pipe the

Oven temperature
220°C/425°F/gas 7

Baking time
7–8 minutes

Baking tins
30 x 38cm (12 x 15in) baking tray, greased, floured, and base-lined; 23 x 6cm (9 x 2½in) spring-form cake tin

Makes
8 servings

Storage
Keeps for 2 days in the refrigerator

✳ Warning
This recipe contains lightly cooked egg whites (see page 9)

mixtures alternately in diagonal lines across the tray (see step 1, below). Dust with icing sugar, wait 5 minutes, then dust again.

6 Bake in the preheated oven for 7–8 minutes. Leave on the tray for a few minutes, then turn out and peel off the paper (see step 2, below).

ASSEMBLING THE DESSERT

1 Measure and cut 2 strips of cake to line the side of the tin. Cut a round to line the base (see step 3, below). Fit the pieces into the tin (see step 4, below). Brush with marmalade.

2 For the chocolate bavarois, put the gelatine and orange juice in a cup and leave for 5 minutes for the gelatine to sponge. Set the cup in hot water until the gelatine has dissolved.

3 Meanwhile, bring the milk to boiling point in a large saucepan. Beat the egg yolks

with 75g (2½oz) of the sugar and the cocoa. Whisk the boiling milk into the egg mixture, then pour back into the saucepan. Cook over a low heat, stirring, until the mixture begins to thicken and just coats the spoon. Do not allow it to come near a simmer, or it will curdle.

4 Remove from the heat and stir in the gelatine and chocolate. Whisk the egg whites and salt until they form soft peaks, add the remaining sugar and whisk for 30 seconds, until the whites are stiff. Fold into the hot chocolate custard.

5 Put the bowl in iced water and turn the mixture occasionally while it thickens. When it starts to set, fold in the whipped cream and liqueur.

6 Pour the bavarois into the cake-lined tin and chill for at least 4 hours. Remove from the tin and decorate with chocolate curls and crystallized peel.

A striped sponge cake case for a rich dessert

How to make the Sponge Case

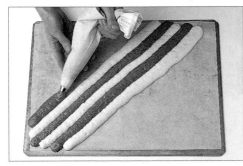

1 To make the striped sponge case, pipe alternate strips of plain and chocolate sponge diagonally across the tray.

2 To peel the baking lining paper neatly off the sponge cake, lift up a corner furthest away from you and peel it back towards you.

3 For the lining, cut strips 6cm (2½in) wide for the side strips; cut the base slightly smaller than that of the 23cm (9in) cake tin.

4 To make the sponge case, fit the side pieces first, trimming to fit, then put in the base piece.

An elegant slice of the Chocolate Bavarois Dessert

Mont Blanc

Another delicious recipe using meringues, this one marries chestnuts and chocolate into a rich, creamy topping for the meringue base.

INGREDIENTS

For the meringues

2 egg whites

pinch of cream of tartar

125g (4oz) caster sugar

½ tsp vanilla extract

For the purée

500g (1lb) vacuum-packed chestnuts

300ml (½ pint) milk

30g (1oz) caster sugar

180g (6oz) plain chocolate, chopped
(see page 32)

1 tsp vanilla extract

300ml (½ pint) double cream, whipped

60g (2oz) plain chocolate, grated
(see page 42)

1 Make the meringue mixture (see page 81), pipe ten circles 7cm (3in) in diameter on the baking sheets, and bake in the preheated oven, all as for Chocolate Meringue Sandwiches (see page 110).

2 Simmer the chestnuts, milk and the sugar together for 10 minutes. Pour into a food processor, add the chocolate and vanilla and process until puréed; alternatively, use a food mill fitted with a large-holed disk.

3 Spoon the purée into a piping bag fitted with a 3mm (⅛in) plain tube. (Add extra milk if the purée seems too thick to pipe). Pipe purée round the edge of each meringue, to make a nest shape. Spoon whipped cream in the centre. Sprinkle grated chocolate over the top. Chill until ready to serve.

VARIATION

Omit the meringue circles and work the purée through a food mill fitted with a large-holed disk directly on to a large serving plate. With the food mill close to the plate, let the strands fall around the outside edge of the dish. Raise the mill as you move toward the centre of the dish, creating a cone-shaped mound. Cover with whipped cream, sprinkle with grated chocolate and serve.

Oven temperature
120°C/250°F/gas ½

Baking time
1–1½ hours

Baking tins
Two flat baking sheets, lined with silicone paper, each marked with five 7cm (3in) circles with 1cm (½in) spaces between

Makes
10

Storage
Purée keeps for 2 days in the refrigerator; complete dessert keeps for 3–4 hours in the refrigerator

Petits Pots au Mocha et Chocolat

Serve these chocolate creams stylishly decorated for maximum effect: the rosette of whipped cream on this mocha petit pot is topped with a coffee bean.

INGREDIENTS

For the mocha petits pots

300ml (½ pint) single cream

2 tbsp medium-ground coffee

60g (2oz) plain chocolate, chopped
(see page 32)

1 tbsp caster sugar

4 egg yolks

For the chocolate petits pots

300ml (½ pint) double cream

180g (6oz) plain chocolate, chopped
(see page 32)

1 teaspoon vanilla extract

1 For the mocha petits pots, bring the cream and ground coffee slowly to the boil, remove from the heat, stir a few times, and strain through a fine sieve or coffee filter paper.

Whisk in the chocolate and sugar until smooth. Whisk in the egg yolks, one at a time.

2 Divide the mixture between 4 ramekins and put in a roasting tin. Pour in hot water to come two-thirds up the sides of the ramekins. Cover the tin with foil. Bake in the preheated oven for about 30 minutes, or until just set. Cool, then chill for 30 minutes before serving.

3 For the chocolate petits pots, bring the cream to the boil, remove from the heat and whisk in the chopped chocolate. When the mixture is smooth, stir in the vanilla. Divide the mixture between 4 ramekins, cool and chill in the refrigerator for at least 3 hours before serving.

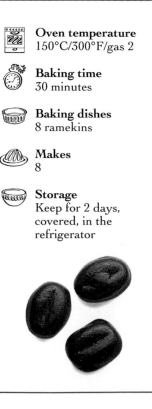

Oven temperature
150°C/300°F/gas 2

Baking time
30 minutes

Baking dishes
8 ramekins

Makes
8

Storage
Keep for 2 days, covered, in the refrigerator

Striped Silk

This elegant dessert requires no decoration other than a pretty serving plate. Serve a sweet biscuit with it, such as chocolate tuiles (see page 89), if liked.

INGREDIENTS

25g (¾oz) gelatine
8 tbsp cold water
1 litre (1¾ pints) milk
8 egg yolks
125g (4oz) caster sugar
60g (2oz) plain chocolate, chopped (see page 32)
2 tsp vanilla extract
45g (1½oz) granulated sugar
350ml (12fl oz) double cream

1 Place the gelatine and 6 tablespoons of the cold water in a cup and leave for 5 minutes for the gelatine to sponge. Set the cup in hot water until the gelatine has dissolved.

2 In a large saucepan, bring the milk to the boil. In a large bowl, whisk the egg yolks with the caster sugar until the mixture is pale yellow. Gradually pour the hot milk over the egg yolks, whisking constantly, then return to the pan and stir with a wooden spoon over low heat until the custard thickens enough to coat the spoon lightly. Do not allow it to come near a simmer or the eggs will curdle. Remove from the heat and stir in the gelatine.

3 Divide the custard between three bowls, preferably stainless steel. Stir the chocolate into one bowl. Add the vanilla essence to the second bowl.

4 Place the granulated sugar in a small heavy-based saucepan and heat until the sugar melts and caramelizes. Swirl the pan when the sugar colours and take it off the heat when it goes a rich brown caramel. The caramel must be well browned or it will be too sweet, but do not let it burn or it will turn bitter. Add the remaining water to the caramel at arm's length to avoid splashes. Stir it over a low heat to blend, then stir it into the third bowl.

5 When the custards have cooled, place the vanilla custard in iced water. When it starts to thicken, fold in one third of the whipped cream.

ASSEMBLING THE MOULD

1 Rinse the mould in cold water and shake out the excess. Spoon in the vanilla cream and chill in the refrigerator or set in the freezer.

2 Set the caramel custard in iced water and when it thickens fold in half of the remaining whipped cream. When the vanilla cream has set, but is not firm, spoon the caramel cream over the top and return the mould to the refrigerator or freezer.

3 Fold the remaining cream into the chocolate custard and spoon it on top of the firm caramel cream. Cover the mould and chill in the refrigerator for at least 4 hours.

SERVING THE STRIPED SILK

1 To serve the Striped Silk, dip the mould in very hot water for a few seconds. Slip a knife around the edge and reverse it on to a serving plate, giving it a good shake if necessary to release the mould. Use a sharp knife when slicing and two spatulas to help slide the slices on to dessert plates.

NOTE: If your mould is a metal one and worn, it may impart a metal taste to the cream. Line it with clingfilm or lightly oiled baking parchment.

Baking dish
2 litre (3½ pint) charlotte or other mould

Makes
12 servings

Storage
Keeps for 2 days, covered, in the refrigerator

Three Chocolate Terrine

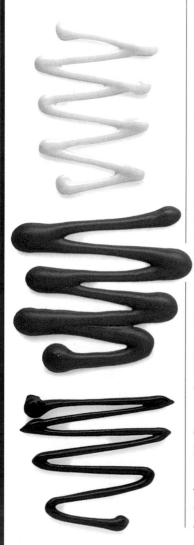

Three layers, three different textures: this terrine uses plain and white chocolate to create the maximum effect.

INGREDIENTS

For the cake layer

60g (2oz) unsalted butter
25g (³/₄oz) cocoa powder
1 egg
100g (3¹/₂oz) caster sugar
¹/₂ tsp vanilla extract
30g (1oz) plain flour

For the white chocolate layer

1 tsp gelatine
6 tbsp cold water
2 tbsp liquid glucose
250g (8oz) white chocolate, chopped (see page 32)
2 egg yolks
pinch of salt
300ml (¹/₂ pint) double cream, lightly whipped

For the plain chocolate layer

1¹/₂ tsp gelatine
3 tbsp cold water
150g (5oz) plain chocolate
2 eggs, separated
2 tbsp rum
pinch of salt
90ml (3fl oz) whipping cream, lightly whipped

1 For the cake layer, melt the butter over a low heat, stir in the cocoa and set aside. Whisk the egg with the caster sugar then stir in the cocoa mixture and the vanilla. Sift the flour over the top and fold in.

2 Pour the mixture into the prepared square cake tin and bake in the preheated oven for 20 minutes. Slide a knife around the inside edge of the tin and leave until cool before turning out on to a wire rack.

3 Cut a piece of cake to fit the bottom of the loaf tin and place in the bottom of the tin.

4 For the white chocolate layer, put the gelatine and 2 tablespoons of the cold water in a cup for 5 minutes for the gelatine to sponge. Put the cup in hot water and leave until the gelatine has dissolved.

5 Bring the remaining water with the glucose to the boil, remove from the heat and stir in the white chocolate and gelatine. When the mixture is smooth, stir in the egg yolks and salt.

6 Lightly whip the cream and carefully fold into the mixture. Pour into the loaf tin and spread level. Chill for about 1 hour, or until nearly set.

7 For the plain chocolate layer, put the gelatine and the water in a cup and leave to sponge. Set the cup in hot water until the gelatine has dissolved.

8 Melt the plain chocolate (see page 33). While it is still hot, stir in the egg yolks and rum. Add the dissolved gelatine. Whisk the egg whites and salt until stiff. Fold into the chocolate. Lightly whip the cream and fold it into the mixture.

9 Spoon the dark chocolate mousse carefully over the white chocolate layer, spread it level, cover with clingfilm and return the loaf tin to the refrigerator for about 8 hours, until the terrine is set.

SERVING THE TERRINE

1 Lift the terrine out of the tin by the clingfilm. Carefully peel away the clingfilm, then cut the terrine into thin slices with a hot, dry knife.

2 Put the slices on dessert plates. If liked, serve with Bitter Chocolate Sauce (see page 135).

Oven temperature
180°C/350°F/gas 4

Baking time
20 minutes

Baking tins
20cm (8in) square cake tin, buttered and floured; 1kg (2lb) loaf tin lined with clingfilm, leaving an overlap at the top

Makes
10–12 servings

Storage
Keeps for 2–3 days, covered, in the refrigerator

Freezing
2 months

Black and White Hazelnut Mousse

Crunchy hazelnut meringue gives extra texture to this layered dessert, which includes two chocolate mousses, dark and white.

INGREDIENTS

For the meringue

125g (4oz) hazelnuts, toasted and skinned (see page 38)
1 tbsp flour
60g (2oz) caster sugar
2 egg whites
pinch of cream of tartar

For the chocolate mousses

1½ tsp gelatine
6 tbsp (90ml) cold water
150g (5oz) white chocolate
2 egg yolks
pinch of salt
180g (6oz) continental plain chocolate
90g (3oz) unsalted butter, cut into small pieces
1 tsp vanilla extract
300ml (½ pint) double cream, lightly whipped

1 For the meringue, grind the nuts with the flour and half the sugar. Whisk the egg whites with the cream of tartar until firm, then whisk in the remaining sugar until they form stiff peaks. Fold in the nut mixture and spread level in the prepared shallow cake tin.

2 Bake in the preheated oven for 20 minutes. Slip a knife around the edge, and leave for 5 minutes. Invert the meringue on to a wire rack, peel off the paper and leave to cool.

3 For the mousses, put the gelatine with 4 tablespoons of the cold water in a cup and leave for 5 minutes for the gelatine to sponge. Put the cup in hot water and leave until the gelatine has dissolved.

4 Melt the white chocolate (see page 33). Stir one egg yolk, a pinch of salt, half the gelatine and the remaining 2 tablespoons of water into the warm, melted white chocolate. Cool in the refrigerator.

5 Melt the plain chocolate (see page 33). Stir the butter, remaining gelatine and egg yolk and the vanilla into the warm, melted chocolate. Chill briefly.

6 Fold half the whipped cream into the white chocolate mixture and half into the plain chocolate mixture.

7 Cut the meringue into two lengths to fit the loaf tin. Put one layer in the tin and spread the dark chocolate cream over the top in an even layer. Put the second meringue on top and spread it with the white chocolate. Cover and chill for at least 5 hours.

8 An hour before serving, remove the mousse from the tin and cut into slices with a hot, dry knife. Put the slices on dessert plates and leave in a cool place. Serve with Raspberry Coulis (see page 137) and fresh raspberries.

Oven temperature
180°C/350°F/gas 4

Baking time
20 minutes

Baking tins
30 x 20cm (12 x 8in) shallow cake tin, lined with silicone paper;
25 x 7cm (10 x 3in) hinged loaf tin, lined with clingfilm, leaving an overlap at the top

Makes
12 servings

Storage
Keeps for 3 days in the refrigerator

Freezing
The mousses freeze for 1–2 months

Step ahead
Make the meringue up to 1 week ahead; store in an airtight container

Marquise au Chocolat Blanc

This recipe combines a light sponge cake with a white chocolate mousse for a light-as-air summertime dessert. Use the egg whites not needed here to make meringues.

* Warning
This recipe contains uncooked egg yolks (see page 9).

INGREDIENTS

For the cake

90g (3oz) plain flour

pinch of salt

3 eggs

90g (3oz) caster sugar

1 tsp vanilla extract

45g (1½oz) butter, melted

For the mousse

1 tsp gelatine

7 tbsp cold water

2 tbsp liquid glucose

300g (10oz) white chocolate, chopped (see page 32)

pinch of salt

3 egg yolks

350ml (12fl oz) double cream

1 For the cake, sift the flour and salt three times. Break the eggs into a large heatproof bowl, and gradually beat in the sugar, using an electric hand-held beater. Set the bowl over hot water and beat for about 8 minutes, until the mixture has doubled in volume.

2 Sift the flour over the mixture, a third at a time, folding in each batch carefully with a large metal spoon. Fold in the vanilla and melted butter.

3 Turn the mixture into the prepared tin and bake in the preheated oven for 35 minutes. Run a knife around the inside of the tin to loosen the cake, leave for 5 minutes, then turn out on to a wire rack to cool.

4 For the mousse, put the gelatine and 2 tablespoons of the water in a cup for 5 minutes to sponge. Put the cup in very hot water and leave until the gelatine has dissolved.

5 Bring the remaining water and the glucose to the boil, remove from the heat and stir in the chocolate, salt and gelatine. When the mixture is smooth, stir in the egg yolks.

6 Lightly whip the cream and carefully fold into the mixture. Pour into the prepared loaf tin and cover with the cake, cut to fit. Chill overnight to set.

7 To serve, turn the marquise out and remove the clingfilm. Cut it into slices with a hot, dry sharp knife. Bitter Chocolate Sauce (see page 135) makes an excellent accompanying sauce.

Oven temperature
180°C/350°F/gas 4

Baking time
35 minutes

Baking tins
20cm (8in) square cake tin, buttered and floured;
500g (1lb) loaf tin lined with clingfilm

Makes
10 servings

Chocolate Cones

These delightfully crisp cones should be filled before serving, in the same way as brandy snaps. Whipped cream, plus a few berry fruits, would be simple but delicious. A more extravagant filling is suggested at the end of the recipe.

INGREDIENTS

50ml (2fl oz) golden syrup

60g (2oz) butter

60g (2oz) caster sugar

45g (1½oz) plain flour

2 tbsp cocoa

1 tbsp lemon juice

1 Melt the syrup, butter and sugar together gently. Sift the flour and cocoa and stir into the mixture. Stir in the lemon juice.

2 Put 5 heaped tablespoons of the mixture on to each of the prepared baking sheets, leaving room for spreading. Bake in batches in the preheated oven for 7–8 minutes per batch.

3 Cool on the baking sheets for 2 minutes. Working quickly, lift off and form into cones round metal or paper cones.

TO FILL THE CONES
For a rich filling, mix 250g (8oz) mascarpone cheese, flavoured with 2 tablespoons sweetened strong coffee, and 150ml (¼ pint) double cream.

Oven temperature
190°C/375°F/gas 5

Baking time
7–8 minutes per batch

Baking tins
Two flat baking sheets, lined with silicone paper

Makes
10 cones

Storage
Keep for 2–3 days in an airtight container

Double Chocolate Festive Dessert

The Festive Dessert cuts easily into elegant slices

Tiny slices of chocolate swiss roll make a pretty tortoiseshell covering for this scrumptious dessert, filled with white chocolate mousse – a special creation for a special occasion.

INGREDIENTS

For the sponge cake

60g (2oz) self-raising flour
30g (1oz) cocoa powder
3 eggs
100g (3½oz) caster sugar

For the apricot filling

1 tsp gelatine
175ml (6 fl oz) cold water
180g (6oz) dried apricots
150ml (¼ pint) whipping cream

For the white chocolate mousse

425g (14oz) white chocolate
125ml (4fl oz) cold water
600ml (1 pint) double cream
2–3 tbsp milk

1 For the sponge cake, sift the flour and cocoa three times. Set aside. Whisk the eggs and sugar in a bowl over a pan of hot water until the mixture is thick and leaves a ribbon trail when the whisk is lifted.

2 Sift the flour mixture over the eggs, a quarter at a time, folding in each addition with a large metal spoon. Pour the batter into the prepared tin and spread level.

3 Bake in the preheated oven for 12–15 minutes. Leave in the tin for a minute or two then turn out on to a piece of silicone paper lightly sprinkled with caster sugar. Peel off the baking paper, lay it back over the cake and replace the tin. Leave for at least 10 minutes.

4 For the apricot filling, put the gelatine and 2 tablespoons of the water in a cup and leave to sponge. Set the cup in hot water and leave until the gelatine dissolves.

5 Simmer the apricots with the remaining water, covered, until the apricots are soft and the water has evaporated. Blend the apricots and gelatine to a purée in a food processor or blender, add the cream and blend again.

ASSEMBLING THE DESSERT

1 Cut the cake into two layers (see page 50). Carefully lift off the top layer and place on a piece of silicone paper. Spread the apricot filling thinly over the cut sides of both layers. Roll each layer of cake tightly from the long side and wrap in the silicone paper. Freeze for several hours or until very firm.

2 Cut the frozen cake into 5mm (¼in) slices, using a sharp knife, and line the prepared mould with them. Press the slices together so there is no space between them. Set the lined mould and any unused slices aside.

3 For the white chocolate mousse, melt the chocolate and water together (see page 34). Leave to cool. Whip the cream to the soft peak stage. Fold the cream carefully into the cooled chocolate, a third at a time, adding the milk if the mixture looks grainy or is difficult to blend.

4 Spoon the mousse into the cake-lined mould. Cover with a layer of the remaining slices of cake and pull over the clingfilm to cover tightly. Chill the dessert for at least 4 hours before serving.

Oven temperature
200°C/400°F/gas 6

Baking time
12 – 15 minutes

Baking tins
31 x 24cm (12½ x 9½in) swiss roll tin, lined with silicone paper;
2 litre (3 pint) pudding bowl or mould, lined with clingfilm (leave an overlap at the top of the bowl)

Makes
14–18 servings

Storage
Keeps for 2 days in the refrigerator

Freezing
2 months

Ice Creams

Ices have been a passion in northern Italy for centuries. From here, Catherine de Medici's chefs brought them to the French court in the 16th century. By the 17th century, the word had spread to England, brought by Italian chefs who were also opening cafés in Paris to sell ices and, later, ice creams. It was Italians, once again, who took ice cream to America early in the 19th century. Today, ice cream is just as much a treat as ever, particularly when it is made at home with real cream and fresh eggs and milk.

Chocolate Praline Ice Cream

An excellent chocolate ice cream to keep in the freezer, this has been given a crunchy texture by the addition of almond praline. If you prefer a smooth ice cream, omit the praline.

INGREDIENTS

100g (3½oz) praline (see page 51)

For the ice cream

180g (6oz) plain chocolate

450ml (¾ pint) milk

5 egg yolks

125g (4oz) caster sugar

300ml (½ pint) double cream, lightly whipped

1 Make the whole praline recipe and store it ready for use. Melt the chocolate (see page 33) and set it aside to cool.

2 Bring the milk to just below boiling point. Whisk the egg yolks with the sugar in a bowl until thick and light, then whisk in the hot milk.

3 Return the mixture to the saucepan and continue to cook over a gentle heat, stirring continuously with a wooden spoon, until the custard thickens enough to coat the spoon and leave a trail when your finger is drawn across the back of the spoon. Do not allow it to come near a simmer or it will curdle.

4 Stir the chocolate into the custard and strain into a bowl. Chill until cool then fold in the whipped cream. Freeze the mixture in an ice cream maker or in the fast-freeze section of a freezer until set, about 3 hours. Before the ice cream has set, stir in 100g (3½oz) of the praline and return to the freezer.

SERVING THE ICE CREAM
For a luxury dessert, serve the ice cream piled in scoops in plain chocolate baskets (see page 44), decorated with piped chocolate fans (see page 47). Add flecks of edible gold foil to the piped decoration.

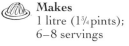

Makes
1 litre (1¾ pints);
6–8 servings

Freezing
2–3 months

Melted plain chocolate pipes easily into decorative shapes

For a sparkling effect, add tiny pieces of edible gold foil

CHOCOLATE PRALINE ICE CREAM
This is a luxurious ice cream, based on an egg custard. Very satisfying served simply, it also lends itself to being turned into an extravagantly presented show-stopper.

Elegantly piped chocolate patterns decorate the ice cream

Chocolate-coated Ice Cream Balls

This is a great excuse for using the ice creams already stored in the freezer.

INGREDIENTS

One quantity
Chocolate Praline Ice Cream
(see page 118)
or *White Chocolate Ice Cream*
(see below),
or a mixture of both

250g (8oz) plain chocolate

1 Put the prepared baking sheet in the freezer for ten minutes. Take small round balls from the ice cream with an ice cream scoop and put them on the cold baking sheet. You should get 24–30 balls.

2 Put the tray back in the freezer until the balls are very hard, about 2–3 hours.

3 Melt half the chocolate (see page 33). Leave until tepid. Roll half the balls, one at a time, in the chocolate. Put back on the baking sheet and return to the freezer as soon as possible.

4 Repeat with the remaining chocolate and ice cream balls, remelting the chocolate if it starts to harden. Serve the balls the day you make them.

Baking tin
Flat baking sheet, lined with silicone paper

Makes
8 servings

White Chocolate Ice Cream

This is a beautifully creamy ice cream. Give it dinner party glamour by serving it in chocolate baskets (see page 44), with piped chocolate fans (see page 46).

INGREDIENTS

375g (12oz) white chocolate

800ml (1⅓ pints) milk

180g (6oz) granulated sugar

3 eggs

1 Melt the chocolate with 6 tablespoons of the milk (see page 34) and set aside. Pour the rest of the milk into a heavy-based saucepan, add half the sugar and slowly bring the mixture to the boil.

2 Meanwhile, beat the eggs and remaining sugar until the mixture is pale and thick. When the milk comes to the boil, pour it over the eggs in a slow steady stream, beating continuously. Return to the saucepan and stir slowly with a wooden spoon, over medium heat, until the custard thickens just enough to coat the spoon and leave a trail when your finger is drawn across the back of the spoon. Do not let the custard come near a simmer or it will curdle.

3 Remove from the heat and whisk in the chocolate. Leave the mixture to cool in an iced water bath.

4 Freeze the cold mixture in an ice-cream maker or in the fast-freeze section of the freezer. Store in the freezer in a covered container until needed.

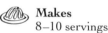
Makes
8–10 servings

Freezing
2–3 months

Chocolate Sorbet

An ice rather than an ice cream, this chocolate sorbet is good served with a sweet biscuit, such as Chocolate Hazelnut Tuiles (see page 89).

INGREDIENTS

500ml (17fl oz) water

125g (4 oz) granulated sugar

60g (2oz) cocoa powder

60g (2oz) continental plain chocolate, chopped (see page 32)

1 Put all the ingredients in a saucepan and bring to the boil, stirring occasionally. Take off the heat and leave to cool.

2 Freeze the mixture in an ice-cream maker or the fast-freeze section of the freezer until set, about 3 hours.

3 Take the mixture from the freezer, chop into several pieces and process in the chilled bowl of a food processor or blender until well blended. Return to the freezer for at least another 2 hours before serving.

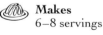
Makes
6–8 servings

Freezing
2–3 months

Chocolate Semifreddo

A generous dash of a coffee-flavoured liqueur, such as Tia Maria, kahlua or crème de café, adds a touch of the exotic to this light chocolate ice.

INGREDIENTS

350ml (12fl oz) double cream
125g (4oz) icing sugar
4 egg whites
90g (3oz) continental plain chocolate, grated
3 tbsp coffee-flavoured liqueur

1 Whip the cream with half the sugar until it forms soft peaks. Whisk the egg whites until stiff, then whisk in the remaining sugar for a few seconds more until they are thick and glossy.

2 Fold the whites into the cream, then fold in the chocolate and liqueur. Spoon the mixture into the prepared tin and spread level. Cover and freeze for at least 8 hours.

3 To serve, lift the Semifreddo out of the tin, using the overlap of clingfilm. Peel off the clingfilm, cut the Semifreddo into slices, and serve on individual plates.

Baking tin
1kg (2lb) loaf tin, lined with clingfilm, leaving a good overlap

Makes
8 servings

Freezing
2 months

＊ Warning
This recipe contains uncooked egg whites (see page 9).

Passion Fruit Surprise Bombe

An ice cream bombe always looks impressive, and this one, made with a delicious passion fruit ice cream, packs an extra surprise.

INGREDIENTS

juice of 1 lemon
125ml (4fl oz) orange juice
1 tsp gelatine
2 egg whites
¼ tsp cream of tartar
180g (6oz) caster sugar
8 passion fruit
300ml (½ pint) double cream
200g (7oz) plain chocolate

1 Strain the lemon juice into a measuring jug. Add enough orange juice to make up to 125ml (4fl oz) of juice. Sprinkle the gelatine over the juice and leave to sponge.

2 Whisk the egg whites with the cream of tartar until they form stiff peaks.

3 Scrape the gelatine mixture into a saucepan, add the sugar and heat gently until dissolved. Increase the heat and boil rapidly for 3 minutes. Pour in a thin stream on to the egg whites, whisking continuously at high speed. Continue whisking for several minutes until cool and thickened.

4 Cut the passion fruit in half, scoop out the insides and put in a blender. Blend for 45 seconds to detach the membranes from the seeds. Strain through a sieve into a bowl, working as much of the juice and pulp through the sieve as possible.

5 Whisk the cream until it is thick but not stiff. Whisk in the passion fruit juice and pulp. Using a large metal spoon, gently fold the cream into the egg white mixture.

6 Transfer to the mould or basin; spread the mixture up the sides, leaving a slight dip in the centre. Freeze for at least 5 hours, until firm.

7 When the ice cream is firm, coarsely grate the chocolate (see page 42). Scoop out the centre of the ice cream and set aside. Fill the cavity with the chocolate. Stir the reserved ice cream to soften it and spread over the chocolate. Return to the freezer for at least one hour.

8 Dip the mould briefly in very hot water, loosen the edges with a thin spatula and turn the bombe out on to a serving plate. Return to the freezer until you are ready to serve it.

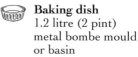
Baking dish
1.2 litre (2 pint) metal bombe mould or basin

Makes
8 servings

Freezing
2 months

Confectionery

The Romans and other early civilizations prepared sweetmeats with fruit juices and honey. In Europe the use of sugar was not widespread until after the Crusades, though by the 15th century, the French were making crystallized fruits and sugared almonds, which they flavoured with musk or amber. The discovery of sugar beet juice, the invention of suitable sweet-making machinery in the 19th century, plus the use of conching to make smooth eating chocolate, combined to give us chocolate confectionery.

Armagnac Prune Truffles

INGREDIENTS

250g (8oz) soft prunes
100ml (3½fl oz) Armagnac
250g (8oz) plain chocolate
250ml (8fl oz) double cream
60g (2oz) unsalted butter

To coat and decorate the truffles

425g (14oz) couverture plain chocolate or 425g (14oz) plain chocolate plus 1 tbsp groundnut or sunflower oil
60g (2oz) plain chocolate
60g (2oz) white chocolate

Armagnac-soaked prunes and plain chocolate are the delectable centres of these chocolate-coated truffles. They make an impressive gift.

1 Put the prunes and the Armagnac in a bowl and leave, covered, for at least 5 days for the prunes to soak in the liqueur.

2 Melt the chocolate, cream and butter together (see page 34). Take off the heat and allow to cool.

3 Strain the prunes, reserving any liquid. Stone the prunes and cut the flesh into pea-size pieces. Stir the prunes into the chocolate mixture and add 2 tablespoons of the soaking liquid. Put a layer of clingfilm over the top of the mixture and chill for 24 hours.

4 Spoon out teaspoonfuls of the chocolate mixture, and lightly roll them into balls between the palms of your hands. Put them on one of the prepared baking sheets and chill for at least one hour before coating them.

5 To coat the truffles, temper the couverture (see page 35), if using, or melt the plain chocolate and oil together (see page 34). The couverture should be at a temperature of 31–32°C (88–90°F) before it is used for coating.

6 Work with a few chocolates at a time, keeping the remainder in the refrigerator. Drop a chocolate into the coating, turning it with a fork to coat all over. Lift it out with the fork, scraping the bottom of the fork against the edge of the pan to remove any excess chocolate. Slide the chocolate on to the second prepared baking sheet.

A selection of the truffles in this chapter, put in a box made from rectangles of marbled chocolate (see pages 45 and 47)

7 Melt the chocolates for the decoration separately(see page 33), put into paper piping bags, and pipe decorative lines on the truffles. Alternatively, top the truffles with walnut pieces.

Baking tins
Two flat baking sheets, lined with silicone paper

Makes
Approx. 1kg (2lbs)

Storage
Keep for 2 weeks in the refrigerator

Step ahead
Begin soaking the prunes in Armagnac five days beforehand

White Chocolate Truffle
(see page 125) with
couverture coating

CHOCOLATE TRUFFLES
*The basic chocolate truffle mixture can
be made into an exciting array of
irresistible sweets. The mixture can be
simply rolled into balls or piped into
pretty shapes, then finished
with a shiny chocolate
covering or rolled in
different coatings.*

Armagnac
Prune Truffle
(see opposite)

Chocolate
Truffle (see
page 124) piped
into a sweet case

Chocolate Truffles

Truffles are sinfully easy to make and warrant the best chocolate you can find. They can be flavoured with your favourite liqueur, and you could add candied orange zest or diced marrons glacés to some of the truffles, instead of the praline suggested in the recipe. Special chocolate bars, such as those flavoured with tea and spices, can also be used for making more unusual truffles.

INGREDIENTS

200ml (7fl oz) single cream
30g (1oz) butter
250g (8oz) continental plain chocolate, broken into pieces
250g (8oz) plain chocolate, broken into pieces
2 tbsp rum, Cognac, or liqueur of your choice (optional)
30g (1oz) praline (see page 51)
To coat the truffles
4 tbsp cocoa powder, sifted with 1 tbsp icing sugar
chocolate vermicelli
praline (see page 51)

1 Heat the cream and the butter in a heavy-based saucepan until it reaches a rolling boil. Remove the mixture from the heat and stir in both chocolates, stirring until the mixture is smooth.

2 Add the liqueur, if using, then pour the mixture into the prepared tin and spread out with a palette knife. Leave in a cool place, uncovered, for 24 hours to firm up.

3 To make the truffles, pull marble-size pieces from the mixture in the tin and roll them in the palms of your hands to shape into balls. Add praline to some of the truffles, if liked.

COATING THE TRUFFLES

1 Prepare the chosen coatings. Sift the cocoa and icing sugar on to silicone or greaseproof paper; sprinkle the other coatings on to flat plates.

2 Roll a few truffles in each coating, using different coatings for different flavours.

PIPING THE TRUFFLES

An alternative way of completing the truffles is to pipe the mixture into foil sweet cases, painted on the inside with a coating of melted chocolate. Put the mixture, while still creamy, into a nylon piping bag fitted with a small star nozzle and pipe it into the cases. Leave to firm up. Peel away the cases.

Baking tin
Shallow cake tin or Swiss roll tin, lined with silicone paper

Makes
Approx. 625g (1¼lb)

Storage
Keep for 2 weeks in the refrigerator, layered between silicone paper in a covered container

Coating truffles in chocolate

1 *Take marble-size pieces of the truffle mixture and roll lightly into balls between the palms of the hands. Ensure your hands are cool and dry.*

2 *To coat a truffle in chocolate, turn it in the melted chocolate with a fork. Lift it from the bowl, scraping the fork against the rim so that excess chocolate falls back into the bowl.*

3 *Put the coated truffles on a piece of silicone or greaseproof paper, spaced well apart, to allow the chocolate to set.*

White Chocolate Truffles

White chocolate truffles have a uniquely rich taste. To keep their creamy colour, try coating them in white couverture or rolling them in finely grated white chocolate, as an alternative to the cocoa suggested here.

INGREDIENTS

180g (6oz) white chocolate, broken into pieces

75g (2½oz) unsalted butter, diced

3 tbsp double cream

pinch of salt

½ teaspoon orange liqueur

2 tbsp sifted cocoa powder, to coat the truffles

1 Melt the chocolate, butter, cream and salt together (see page 34). Remove from the heat and leave to cool. When the mixture has cooled add the liqueur. Cover and chill in the refrigerator until firm, about 2 hours.

2 Pull marble-sized pieces off the chilled mixture and roll them in the palms of your hands to shape into balls. If the mixture becomes difficult to handle, return to the refrigerator and chill further.

3 Put the cocoa on a piece of greaseproof paper; roll the truffles in it to coat them evenly.

 Makes Approx. 30

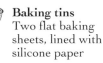 **Storage** Keep for 2 weeks in the refrigerator, layered between silicone paper in a covered container

Chocolate-covered Nuts

Chocolate and nuts are a wonderful combination. Pecans, almonds and walnuts are particularly good if they are caramelized before being coated with chocolate. I tell you how to do this at the end of this recipe.

INGREDIENTS

750g (1½lbs) couverture chocolate or 750g (1½ lbs) plain chocolate and 1 tbsp sunflower or groundnut oil

375g (12oz) toasted and skinned hazelnuts (see page 38) or macadamia nuts

1 Temper the couverture (see page 35) or melt the plain chocolate and oil together (see page 34). For best results, the couverture chocolate should be 31°–32°C (88°–90°F) before being used for coating.

2 Make a large paper piping bag (see page 46) and fill it with some of the melted chocolate. Snip a hole in the cone and squeeze out 40 half-teaspoon-size drops on to one of the prepared baking sheets.

3 Arrange three nuts in a triangle on top of each chocolate drop and leave to set.

4 Remelt the remaining chocolate, if necessary. Using a fork, submerge a nut cluster in the chocolate. Lift out and scrape gently on the edge of the bowl to shake any excess chocolate back into the bowl.

5 Put the nut clusters on the second prepared baking sheet to dry. Repeat with the remaining nuts.

NOTE
To caramelize nuts, heat 250g (8oz) sugar in a heavy-based saucepan, stirring continuously, until pale caramel in colour. Take the pan off the heat and use a fork to dip the nuts, one at a time, in the hot syrup. Lay them on a lightly oiled baking sheet to set.

If the caramel becomes too thick, reheat it over a very low heat. The caramelized nuts must be cold before being used in the recipe above.

 Baking tins Two flat baking sheets, lined with silicone paper

Makes Approx. 40

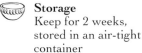 **Storage** Keep for 2 weeks, stored in an air-tight container

Panforte di Siena

Panforte – the Italian word translates as "hard bread" – is really a sweet, and a very special one, packed full of nuts, honey, candied peel and spices. In Siena the windows of many shops are stacked high with beautifully wrapped discs of Panforte. It keeps well and makes an attractive gift, particularly when wrapped in Florentine-style paper.

INGREDIENTS

125g (4oz) candied orange
and lemon peel, chopped

2 tbsp brandy

125g (4oz) unblanched almonds

125g (4oz) unblanched hazelnuts

125g (4oz) plain flour

2 tbsp cocoa powder

2 tsp ground cinnamon

½ tsp ground coriander

½ tsp ground allspice

150g (5oz) granulated sugar

150ml (¼ pint) dark runny honey

1 tbsp icing sugar mixed
with ½ tsp cinnamon

1 Mix the peel and brandy in a mixing bowl and set aside.

2 Bring a small saucepan of water to the boil. Add the almonds and bring back to the boil. Lift an almond out with a slotted spoon and squeeze it to see if it will peel easily. If it does, drain and peel the almonds. If it doesn't, boil for another minute; peel the almonds.

3 Place the almonds in one shallow tin and the hazelnuts in another and bake in an oven preheated to the higher temperature for about 8 minutes. Shake the pans occasionally so the nuts toast evenly. Remove the nuts from the oven; reduce the oven temperature to the lower setting. Rub the hazelnuts in a cloth to remove the skins.

4 Chop the hazelnuts and the almonds very roughly and mix into the peel. Sift the flour, cocoa and spices together and stir into the peel.

5 Put the sugar and honey into a small, heavy-based saucepan. Stir over low heat until the syrup comes to the boil, then boil without stirring until the syrup reaches 127°C (260°F), measured on a sugar thermometer.

6 Pour the hot syrup over the nut and peel mixture and stir to blend. Pour into the prepared tin and bake for 40 minutes. Remove from the oven and set on a wire rack to cool.

7 When partially cool, sprinkle with the icing sugar and cinnamon. Remove the Panforte from the tin when cold and leave in a dry place for several days to firm up. It should be chewy but firm enough to stay flat and be cut into slices.

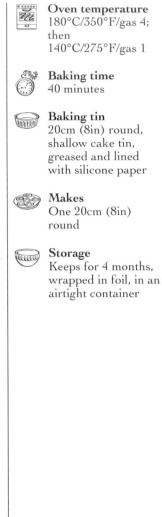

Oven temperature
180°C/350°F/gas 4;
then
140°C/275°F/gas 1

Baking time
40 minutes

Baking tin
20cm (8in) round,
shallow cake tin,
greased and lined
with silicone paper

Makes
One 20cm (8in)
round

Storage
Keeps for 4 months,
wrapped in foil, in an
airtight container

Rocky Road

Children enjoy this American candy made with milk chocolate, nuts and marshmallows. The bumpy surface explains the name.

INGREDIENTS

12 marshmallows

90g (3oz) walnuts or pecan nuts

500g (1lb) milk chocolate, chopped
(see page 32)

1 Dice the marshmallows and roughly chop the nuts. Melt the chocolate (see page 33).

2 Stir the marshmallows and nuts into the chocolate and pour on to the prepared baking sheet. With a lightly oiled palette knife, smooth over the surface, covering any nuts and marshmallows with the chocolate.

3 Leave the mixture to set for 1–1½ hours in the refrigerator before breaking it into small pieces.

VARIATION

Substitute 125g (4oz) dried banana chips for the marshmallows and nuts and follow the recipe.

Baking tin
Flat baking sheet,
lined with silicone
paper

Makes
Approx. 625g (1¼lb)

Storage
Keeps for 2 weeks in
the refrigerator

Chocolate Buttercrunch

When I was a teenager living in New York City there was a chain of confectionery shops called Loft's that made a delicious buttercrunch candy. Years later, I was delighted to find I could make this very similar version.

INGREDIENTS

250g (8oz) unblanched almonds

250g (8oz) granulated sugar

4 tbsp water

250g (8oz) unsalted butter, cut into small pieces

1 tbsp lemon juice

250g (8oz) plain chocolate

1 Finely chop one third of the nuts and set aside. Roughly chop the remaining two thirds.

2 Place the sugar and water in a heavy-based saucepan and stir over a low heat until the sugar has almost dissolved. Add the butter and continue to stir until the mixture has blended.

3 Add the roughly chopped nuts and cook over a moderate heat, stirring occasionally, until the mixture reaches 150°C (300°F), measured on a sugar thermometer.

4 The syrup should turn a caramel colour, but it must be watched with great care at this stage to prevent it catching and burning.

5 The moment the mixture reaches the correct temperature, remove it from the heat, stir in the lemon juice, and quickly pour it into the prepared tin.

6 Before the buttercrunch sets, lift it out of the tin and score the top into 4cm (1½in) squares with a sharp knife. When it is cold, carefully peel away the lining paper and cut or break the buttercrunch into neat squares.

7 Melt the chocolate (see page 33). Spread the reserved finely chopped nuts on a square of greaseproof paper. Spread the tops of the squares with chocolate, then press into the nuts. Cover the bottoms of the buttercrunch in the same way.

8 Allow the chocolate to set before storing the buttercrunch, between layers of silicone or greaseproof paper, in an airtight container.

Baking tin
20cm (8 in) square cake tin, base and sides lined with silicone paper

Makes
Approx. 625g (1¼lb)

Storage
Keeps for 2 weeks in an airtight container

Chocolate Pomelo Candies

The pomelo (also called shaddock) is a very large citrus fruit. Its peel is particularly good for candying. Its flavour is intense and, once candied, it has an attractive translucent appearance.

INGREDIENTS

2 pomelos or grapefruit or 3 large oranges

1 litre (1¾ pints) water

500g (1lb) granulated or caster sugar

180g (6oz) plain chocolate

1 Wash and dry the fruit. Use a small sharp knife to make 4 slits from the top to bottom at quarterly intervals. Remove the peel in neat leaf-shaped sections. Put the peel in a saucepan, cover with plenty of boiling water, and simmer for 10 minutes. Refresh in cold water, then repeat the boiling and refreshing process as many times as necessary to reduce the citrus bitterness to a level you find palatable.

2 Dissolve the sugar in the water over a low heat, add the peel and simmer gently for 1½ hours, until the peel is soft. Remove the peel from the syrup and put on a wire rack to dry. Drain in a strainer, then on paper until cool.

3 Melt the chocolate (see page 33). Cut the peel into thin batons. Spear each piece of peel with a wooden toothpick and dip it in the chocolate, either halfway or to coat the whole piece. Stick the toothpick into a potato until the chocolate sets.

Makes
500g (1lb)

Storage
Keep for 3 weeks in an airtight container

Peppermint Creams

A favourite after-dinner treat. Oil of peppermint, which can be bought at chemists, gives a result far superior to that of peppermint flavouring.

INGREDIENTS

375g (12oz) granulated sugar

125ml (4 fl oz) water

1 tsp lemon juice

6 – 8 drops oil of peppermint

plain chocolate for coating (see Armagnac Prune Truffles, page 122)

1 Put the sugar, water and lemon juice in a heavy-based saucepan. Stir carefully over moderate heat to dissolve the sugar. Brush down the sides of the pan with a pastry brush dipped in water to dissolve any grains of sugar.

2 Boil until the syrup reaches 115°C (240°F), measured on a sugar thermometer. Remove from the heat and add the peppermint oil.

3 Pour on to a damp work surface. Allow to cool for several minutes before working with a damp spatula in a figure-of-eight motion. Work the mixture for about 10 minutes, until it becomes opaque and stiffens slightly. If the mixture is still quite soft, leave for 30 minutes to become firmer.

4 Drop teaspoonfuls of the fondant on silicone paper. Set aside until cold.

5 Coat the fondants in plain chocolate, as for Armagnac Prune Truffles (see page 122).

Makes
Approx. 500g (1lb)

Storage
Keep for 2 weeks in an airtight container

Chocolate Mint Crisps

These can be whipped up in minutes and are quite perfect to serve with after-dinner coffee.

INGREDIENTS

125g (4oz) plain chocolate

6 drops oil of peppermint

1 tbsp demerara sugar

1 Melt the chocolate (see page 33). Leave until it is slightly cool to the touch but still liquid. Add the oil of peppermint and the sugar. Taste, adding more oil of peppermint if you want the crisps to have a stronger, more minty flavour.

2 Pour the mixture on to the prepared baking sheet and spread out to make a rectangle measuring about 16 x 23 cm (6½ x 9in). Before it sets, score the chocolate into 3.5cm (1½in) squares. When it is firm and cool, cut it into squares.

Baking tin
Two flat baking sheets, lined with silicone paper

Makes
Approx. 24

Storage
Keep for 2 weeks in an airtight container

Chocolate Fudge

Fudge is always a great favourite with children – and with adults.

INGREDIENTS

425g (14oz) granulated sugar

250ml (8 fl oz) milk

1 tbsp liquid glucose

90g (3oz) unsalted butter

60g (2oz) plain chocolate

45g (1½oz) cocoa powder

1 tsp vanilla extract

60g (2oz) walnuts, chopped

1 Put the sugar, milk and glucose into a heavy-based saucepan and stir together over moderate heat until the sugar dissolves. Cook without stirring until the temperature reaches 114°C (238°F), measured on a sugar thermometer.

2 Meanwhile, melt the butter, chocolate and cocoa together (see page 34). When the syrup has reached the correct temperature pour in the chocolate mixture. Stir in the vanilla and nuts and pour into the prepared tin.

3 Cut the fudge into small squares when it has set.

Baking tin
20 x 20cm (8 x 8in) square shallow cake tin, lined with silicone paper

Makes
Approx. 625g (1¼lb)

Storage
Keeps for 2 weeks in an airtight container

Chocolate Eggs

You can present these chocolate-filled egg shells innocently masquerading as fresh hens' eggs. To make an assortment of chocolate eggs, use plastic egg moulds, available in various sizes. The moulds can be filled with alternate spoonfuls of white and plain chocolate to give a marbled effect. Once unmoulded, the egg halves can be stuck together with a little melted chocolate.

INGREDIENTS

6 small eggs

300g (10oz) continental plain chocolate

175ml (6 fl oz) double cream

90g (3oz) praline, finely ground, (see page 51)

2 tbsp white rum (optional)

1 With a needle, pierce a small hole in the pointed end of each egg. Use small scissors to enlarge the hole to a circle about 1cm (½in) in diameter. Shake the raw egg out into a bowl and reserve for another use. Pour running water into the shells and shake until they are clean and empty. Dry the shells in a low oven for 10 minutes.

2 Melt the chocolate (see page 33). Bring the cream to the boil in a small saucepan, remove from the heat and stir in the chocolate. Stir in the praline and rum. Spoon or pipe the mixture into the egg shells until full. Wipe any chocolate off the outer shells and chill until firm. Seal the holes with a small round label and place in an egg box or small basket with the labels at the bottom.

VARIATION
Crack the shells of the filled eggs and peel off. Decorate the chocolate eggs with narrow ribbons, or wrap them in coloured foil.

Makes
6 eggs

Storage
Keep for 2 weeks in the refrigerator

Marbled Chocolate Eggs, made in plastic moulds, sit in a nest of chocolate curls

Savoury Chocolate

Chocolate was first used in South America as a drink spiced with chillies. Even after the Spanish sweetened its naturally bitter flavour, chocolate continued to be used in Europe, particularly in Italy and Spain, to enhance certain savoury dishes. The recipes here, which come from Europe and Mexico, show the great versatility of chocolate as a savoury ingredient, combining it with poultry, game and seafood, as well as the Aztecs' chillies.

Mole de Guajolote

The word mole, from the Mexican Indian word molli, means a sauce made from chillies. I have chosen a moderately hot version, but you can easily raise or lower the heat by adjusting the amount of chillies.

Enhance the flavour of the chillies by heating them before soaking overnight. Heat in a heavy-based pan for 3 minutes to soften them.

INGREDIENTS

6 mulato chillies, deseeded
6 ancho chillies, deseeded
4 pasilla chillies, deseeded
4kg (8lb) turkey, cut into portions
1 onion, quartered
5 garlic cloves, crushed
1½ tsp salt
60g (2oz) sesame seeds
125g (4oz) blanched almonds
2 corn or flour tortillas
3 mild onions, chopped
5 tomatoes, skinned and chopped
60g (2oz) raisins
6 black peppercorns
2 cloves
½ tsp aniseed
1 tsp ground cinnamon
4–6 tbsp sunflower oil
60–90g (2–3oz) plain chocolate
salt and freshly ground black pepper

1 Soak the chillies overnight in 900ml (1½ pints) water.

2 Put the turkey pieces in a large saucepan with the onion and 2 garlic cloves, cover with water and bring to the boil. Add the salt, cover and simmer 1 hour, or until the turkey is just tender.

3 Cool, then take the turkey pieces out of the casserole, skin them and cut the meat off the bones into neat pieces. Put the meat into a large flame-proof casserole. Return the skin and bones to the pan and simmer for another hour to concentrate the stock's flavour.

4 Set aside a few sesame seeds for garnish and toast the rest with the almonds in a dry frying pan, tossing them over a moderate heat until browned. Remove, then cook the tortillas in the hot pan for about 5 minutes, turning them, until they are hard and brittle. Break them into small pieces.

5 Put the soaked chillies and their water, the mild onions, remaining garlic, tomatoes and tortillas in a processor or blender and work to a smooth paste. Transfer to a bowl.

6 Rinse out and dry the processor or blender and add the sesame seeds, almonds, raisins, peppercorns and spices. Grind the mixture finely, then add it to the chilli paste.

7 Heat the oil in a large sauté pan and fry the paste, stirring continuously, for about 5 minutes. Add to the casserole.

8 Measure out 600ml (1 pint) of the stock and put it in a pan with the chocolate, broken into pieces. Heat until the chocolate has dissolved; pour into the casserole. Season to taste with salt and pepper. Simmer gently over a very low heat, adding more stock if necessary, until the sauce is the consistency of double cream.

Makes
12 servings

Storage
Keeps for 7 days in the refrigerator

Freezing
2–3 months

MOLE DE GUAJOLOTE *is one of Mexico's most renowned dishes. The recipe on these pages is a version of one served by the great Aztec Emperor Montezuma.*

SERVING THE MOLE DE GUAJOLOTE

Garnish the dish with the reserved sesame seeds or a green herb and serve it with white rice, cooked beans and warm soft tortillas. Extra garnishes such as avocados, limes and chillies add an exotic, colourful touch.

Vivid green flat-leaf parsley garnishes this Mexican dish

Venison Stew

A wonderful winter dish and special enough to be party fare. It improves with reheating, so can be made well in advance. It also makes an excellent filling for pies.

INGREDIENTS

1.25kg (2½lb) venison meat from the shoulder, off the bone

For the marinade

2 tbsp olive oil

1 carrot, chopped

1 large onion, sliced

1 stalk celery, chopped

375ml (13fl oz) red wine

For the stew

2 tbsp olive oil

4 shallots, finely chopped

4 garlic cloves, crushed and chopped

300ml (½ pint) beef stock

1 tbsp tomato purée

bouquet garni, made up of one bay leaf, sprig of thyme, several stalks of parsley

10 juniper berries

10 peppercorns

strip of orange peel

1½ tbsp redcurrant jelly

45g (1½oz) continental plain chocolate, grated (see page 42)

salt and freshly ground black pepper

1 Cut the meat into small cubes and put in a bowl.

2 For the marinade, heat the oil in a large frying pan and gently fry the carrot, onion and celery until lightly browned. Pour in the wine and remove from the heat. When the marinade is cool pour it over the meat. Leave overnight in a cool place or in the refrigerator.

3 Next day, lift the venison out of the marinade and pat it dry with kitchen paper. Reserve the marinade.

4 For the stew, heat the oil in a non-stick pan and brown the meat, in batches, on all sides. Remove the meat to a heatproof casserole. Add the shallots and garlic to the pan and stir over the heat until softened. Add them to the casserole.

5 Pour the marinade, with its vegetables, into the frying pan and stir, scraping up any brown bits from the bottom of the pan. Tip the marinade into the casserole and add the stock, tomato purée, bouquet garni, juniper berries, peppercorns and orange peel.

6 Season lightly with salt, bring to a simmer on top of the stove, cover, and put in the preheated oven. Adjust the heat, if necessary, so the stew cooks very slowly – a bare simmer – for about 2–2½ hours, until the meat is tender.

7 Strain the juices into a saucepan. Boil briskly to reduce by one quarter. Whisk in the redcurrant jelly and the chocolate. Add pepper (and extra salt, to taste). Pour the sauce back over the stew and remove the bouquet garni. Serve it hot. A swede or parsnip purée, chestnuts and a green vegetable go well with this stew.

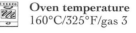

Oven temperature
160°C/325°F/gas 3

Cooking time
2–2½ hours

Makes
6 servings

Storage
Keeps for 2–3 days, covered, in the refrigerator

Calamares con Chocolate

The original Catalan dish on which this recipe is based uses baby octopus (pulpitos) but the more readily available squid is a good substitute.

INGREDIENTS

750g (1½lb) squid
3 tbsp olive oil
2 garlic cloves
25g (¾oz) flaked almonds
1 large mild onion, finely chopped
1 bay leaf
½ teaspoon dried thyme
250ml (8fl oz) white wine
4 tomatoes, skinned and chopped
pinch saffron
15g (½oz) continental plain chocolate, grated (see page 42)
2 tbsp finely chopped parsley
salt and freshly ground black pepper

1 To prepare each squid, hold the sac firmly and pull off the head and tentacles. Cut the tentacles off and reserve. Extract the long bone from the sac and any gelatinous matter and discard. Rinse the sac under cold running water. Cut the sac into rings and the tentacles into pieces.

2 Heat 2 tablespoons of the oil in a sauté or frying pan and fry the garlic and almonds until lightly browned. Transfer them to a mortar. Add the remaining oil to the pan and soften the onion in it, then add the squid, bay leaf and thyme. When the squid turns opaque pour in the wine. Reduce the sauce slightly, then add the tomatoes and salt and pepper. Cover, and simmer gently until the squid is tender, about 1 hour.

3 Pound the almonds and garlic with the saffron to make a paste, thinning it with a little of the pan juices. Stir the paste into the squid, add the chocolate and let the mixture heat through to thicken. Stir in the parsley. Serve with boiled new potatoes, to soak up the fragrant sauce.

Makes
4 servings

Storage
Keeps for 2–3 days, covered, in the refrigerator

Freezing
2–3 months

Conejo con Chocolate

Plain chocolate is used frequently to flavour game sauces in Spain. The amount of chocolate is relatively small but it imparts a subtle, although difficult to identify, taste.

INGREDIENTS

4 tbsp olive oil
2 garlic cloves
1 rabbit, jointed
seasoned flour for coating
1 onion, sliced
1 carrot, sliced
sprig of thyme
1 bay leaf
small piece cinnamon stick
300ml (½ pint) red wine
1 small glass dry sherry
45g (1½oz) blanched almonds
45g (1½oz) pine nuts
30g (1oz) continental plain chocolate, chopped (see page 32)
2 tbsp brandy
pinch of sugar (optional)
salt and freshly ground black pepper

1 Heat the oil in a casserole and fry the garlic until lightly coloured. Transfer with a slotted spoon to a mortar and set aside.

2 Toss the rabbit in the flour and fry until browned. Add the onion, carrot, thyme, bay leaf and cinnamon. Stir briefly to distribute the vegetables then pour in the wine and sherry. Season with salt and pepper. Bring to the boil and simmer gently, covered, for 40 minutes.

3 Pound the garlic with the almonds, pine nuts and chocolate, and a few tablespoons of pan juices, if necessary, to make a paste. Dilute with the brandy. Add to the rabbit and simmer a few minutes more. Taste for seasoning, adding a pinch of sugar if the sauce is too bitter. Serve with rice or potatoes.

Makes
4 servings

Storage
Keeps for 2–3 days, covered, in the refrigerator

Freezing
2–3 months

Sauces & Fillings

Add a richly flavoured chocolate filling to a cake or a smooth sauce to a dessert and you immediately lift them out of the everyday into the luxury class. The chocolate sauces and fillings here are perfect with chocolate-based recipes, but would also add an extra dimension to recipes that do not contain chocolate. As with any chocolate recipe, the success of a chocolate sauce or filling depends on the quality of the chocolate used. Always choose a chocolate with a high cocoa solid content and not too much sugar in it.

Chocolate Sauce

Here is an easy alternative to the Bitter Chocolate Sauce opposite. This one is made with cocoa powder.

INGREDIENTS
60g (2oz) cocoa powder

250ml (8fl oz) water

125g (4oz) caster sugar

30g (1oz) butter

Simmer the cocoa, water and sugar together, stirring, for 3 minutes. Stir in the butter, and return to a simmer. Add more water, if necessary, to make a pouring consistency.

Makes
300ml (½ pint)

Storage
Keeps 2–3 days, covered, in the refrigerator

Crème Anglaise

Crème Anglaise, a light soothing custard, is very good served with a variety of chocolate desserts. It is also the base for many ice creams. It has to be made with care to ensure that the egg yolks, which thicken the milk, do not curdle.

INGREDIENTS
300ml (½ pint) milk

½ vanilla pod, split in two or 1 tsp vanilla extract

3 egg yolks

25g (1oz) caster sugar

1 Bring the milk almost to the boil, with the vanilla pod, if you are using it.

2 Beat the egg yolks with the sugar until thick and light, then whisk in the hot milk. Return the mixture to the pan and cook over a low heat, stirring constantly with a wooden spoon, until the cream thickens slightly. Do not allow the mixture to come near a simmer or it will curdle.

3 Strain into a bowl and leave to cool, when it will thicken more. Add the vanilla extract, if using it, and refrigerate.

VARIATIONS:
Coffee Crème Anglaise: Add a tablespoon of instant coffee, diluted in a little water, to the basic Crème Anglaise.
Mocha Crème Anglaise: Add 60g (2oz) grated plain chocolate and 1 teaspoon instant coffee to the cream when it is thickened.
Liqueur Crème Anglaise: Add a tablespoon or more to taste of Poire William or Grand Marnier.

Makes
350ml (12fl oz)

Storage
Keeps 2–3 days in the refrigerator

Hot Fudge Sauce

This has a fine fudgy flavour, and is as good poured over ice creams as it is with hot puddings.

INGREDIENTS
125ml (4fl oz) whipping cream

30g (1oz) unsalted butter

45g (1½oz) cocoa powder, sifted

60g (2oz) caster sugar

60g (2oz) soft dark brown sugar

pinch of salt

Place all the ingredients in a heavy-based saucepan. Stir over gentle heat until the mixture is smooth and melted. Increase the heat slightly and continue to cook the sauce for 2–3 minutes. If a sweeter sauce is desired, add more caster sugar.

Makes
150ml (¼ pint)

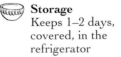
Storage
Keeps 1–2 days, covered, in the refrigerator

*Bitter Chocolate
Sauce served with
a steamed pudding*

CHOCOLATE SAUCES

*Smooth, creamy sauces made with
chocolate add an extra pleasure to
many kinds of dessert. Serve them
warm with steamed puddings or hot
pies and tarts, and cool with ice
creams and fruits.*

Bitter Chocolate Sauce

INGREDIENTS

*100g (3½oz) continental plain chocolate
or bitter dessert chocolate*

30g (1oz) unsalted butter

5 tbsp water

1 tbsp rum or brandy

Melt the first three ingredients
together in a small heavy-based
saucepan over gentle heat,
stirring constantly. When the
ingredients are smooth, stir in
the alcohol. Serve the sauce
cold or warm.

Makes
300ml (½ pint)

Storage
Keeps 1–2 days,
covered, in the
refrigerator

Chocolate Ganache

This versatile chocolate cream can be used as a filling, an icing and a sauce.

INGREDIENTS

150g (5oz) continental plain chocolate, chopped (see page 32)

150g (5oz) plain chocolate, chopped (see page 32)

300ml (½ pint) double cream

1 Put the chocolate in a large bowl. Bring the cream to the boil, pour over the chocolate and leave for 5 minutes. Whisk gently until the cream and chocolate are blended.

2 Continue to whisk until the ganache is fluffy and cool. Do not overbeat or it will be too stiff to spread. If the ganache is to be used as a sauce, whisk only until it is blended and still warm.

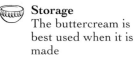

Makes
Enough to fill and ice a 23cm (9in) two-layer cake; serves 8 as a sauce

Storage
Keeps for 2–3 days in the refrigerator

Chocolate Buttercream

Buttercream makes an excellent filling and icing for layer cakes. Its basic ingredients, as used in the Wedding Cake on page 66, are egg yolks, butter, water and sugar. Here, I give a recipe for a plain chocolate buttercream. For a white chocolate buttercream, see the recipe for White Chocolate Cake (page 61).

INGREDIENTS

4 egg yolks

125g (4 oz) granulated sugar

100ml (3½floz) water

250g (8oz) unsalted butter, chopped

100g (3½oz) continental plain chocolate, melted (see page 33)

1 Beat the egg yolks in a bowl until they are pale and thick.

2 Gently heat the sugar and water in a heavy-based saucepan until dissolved. Bring to the boil and boil until the syrup reaches the soft ball stage, 115°C (240°F), measured on a sugar thermometer.

3 Gradually pour the syrup over the egg yolks, beating with a hand-held electric mixer (avoid pouring the syrup over the beater's blades) until the mixture is thickened and tepid.

4 Beat the softened butter gradually into the mixture. Mix in the melted chocolate.

Makes
Enough to fill and ice a 23cm (9in) two-layer cake

Storage
The buttercream is best used when it is made

Chocolate Glaze

This is a rich, glossy icing for cakes. A simpler icing, based on cocoa, is given with the recipe for Eclairs (see page 85).

INGREDIENTS

90g (3oz) continental plain chocolate

90g (3oz) plain chocolate

125g (4oz) unsalted butter

1 tbsp golden syrup

1 Break both of the chocolates into small pieces.

2 Melt the chocolate pieces with the other ingredients in a heavy-based saucepan (see page 34).

3 Sit the cake to be glazed on a wire rack over a large plate and pour the glaze over (see page 49).

Makes
Enough to glaze a 20–23cm (8–9in) cake

Apricot Filling

This creamy, fruity filling is excellent with chocolate cakes and roulades. Dried apricots have a high sugar content, so no extra sugar is needed here.

INGREDIENTS

1 tsp gelatine

175ml (6fl oz) water

180g (6oz) dried apricots

150ml (¼ pint) whipping cream

1 Put the gelatine and 2 tablespoons of the water in a cup and leave to sponge. Put the cup in a bowl of hot water until the gelatine has dissolved.

2 Place the apricots with the remaining water in a heavy-based saucepan. Cover the pan, then simmer until the apricots are soft and the water has evaporated.

3 Blend the apricots and gelatine to a purée in a food processor, then add the cream to the mixture and blend again for a smooth filling.

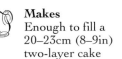

Makes
Enough to fill a 20–23cm (8–9in) two-layer cake

Raspberry Coulis

This sharp and fruity red sauce is delicious with all kinds of chocolate confections. It should be kept on the tart side to balance the sweetness of the dessert.

INGREDIENTS

300g (10oz) raspberries, fresh or frozen

90g (3oz) caster sugar

1 Put the raspberries and sugar in a bowl. Leave for at least 1 hour to allow the flavours time to develop.

2 Blend the fruit and sugar to a purée in a food processor (or beat with a whisk).

3 Rub the mixture through a fine sieve into a bowl, and press as much of the juice through as possible. Serve the coulis cold.

Makes
300ml (½ pint)

Storage
Keeps for 2 days in the refrigerator

Freezing
2 months

Orange Sauce

A quick sauce can be made from the fresh blood orange juice now available in cartons. It has a strong, tart flavour that goes well with cakes or puddings rich in chocolate.

INGREDIENTS

2 tsp cornflour

2 tbsp water

300ml (½ pint) freshly squeezed blood orange juice

sugar to taste, optional

1 Put the cornflour and water in a bowl and mix to a smooth paste.

2 Pour the orange juice into a small, heavy-based saucepan. Stir in the cornflour paste.

3 Bring the mixture to a simmer, stirring constantly. Add sugar to taste, if needed. The sauce is best used as soon as it is made.

Makes
300ml (½ pint)

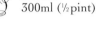

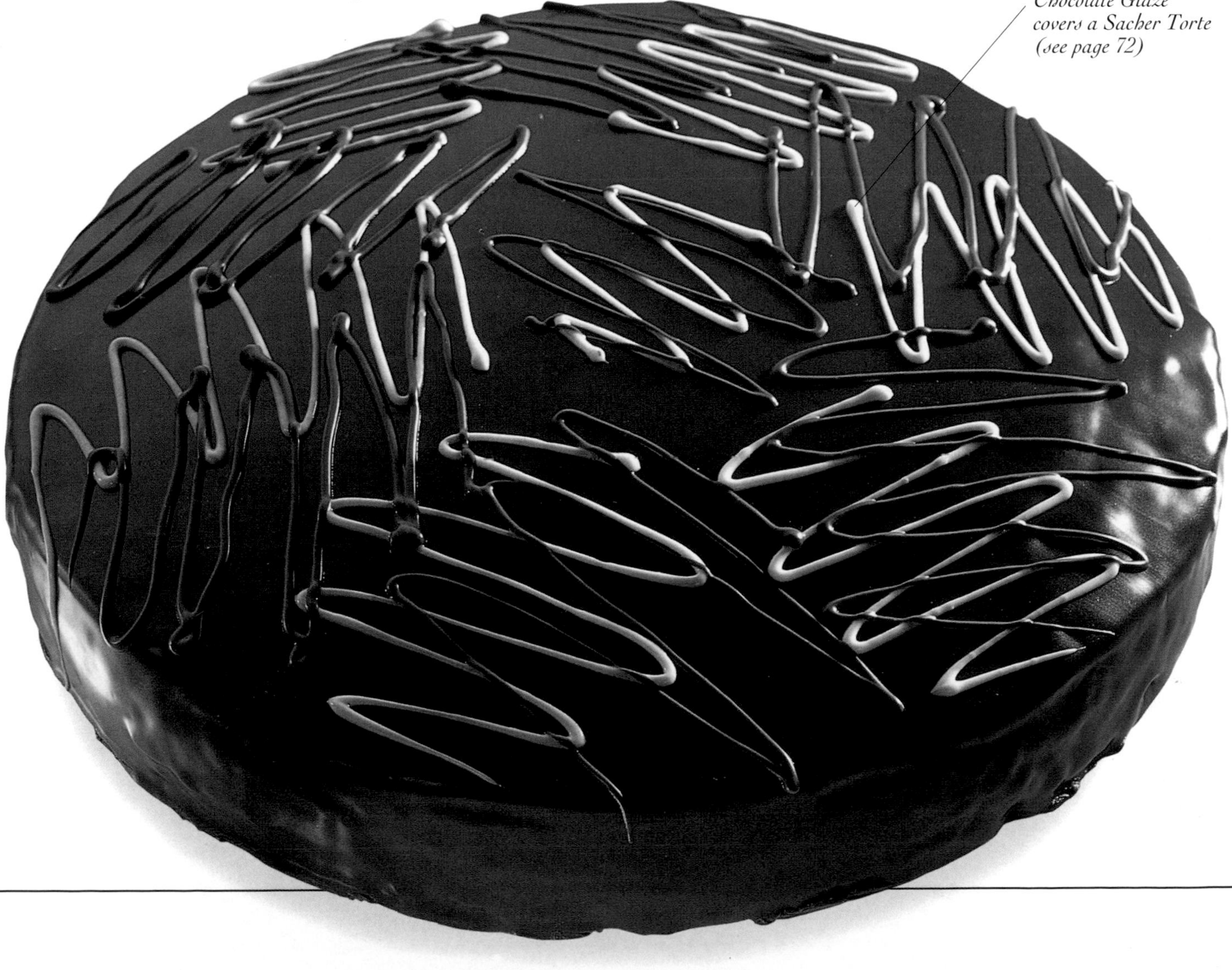

Chocolate Glaze covers a Sacher Torte (see page 72)

Chocolate Drinks

" 'Monsieur,' Madame d'Arestel, Superior of the Convent of the Visitation at Belley, once said to me more than fifty years ago, 'whenever you want to make a really good cup of chocolate, make it the day before, in a porcelain coffee-pot, and let it set. The night's rest will concentrate it and give it a velvety quality which will make it better. Our good God cannot possibly take offence at this little refinement, since he himself is everything that is most perfect'." – J.A. Brillat-Savarin, *Physiologie du goût*, 1825.

Viennese Hot Chocolate

This delicious drink conjures up thoughts of the great days of the Austro-Hungarian Empire, when Vienna was the liveliest city in Europe.

INGREDIENTS
150ml (¼ pint) double cream

900ml (1½ pints) milk

3 tbsp caster sugar

1 tbsp dark rum or cognac

250g (8oz) continental plain chocolate, finely chopped (see page 32)

1 Lightly whip the cream and set aside.

2 Heat the milk in a large saucepan until almost boiling. Remove from the heat and whisk in the sugar, rum or cognac, and all but a tablespoon of the chocolate.

3 Ladle into 4 cups and top with a dollop of whipped cream and a sprinkling of the remaining chocolate.

VARIATION
Mexican Hot Chocolate
For this version, omit the cream and stir in a pinch of ground cloves and half a teaspoon of ground cinnamon.

Makes
4 servings

Chocolate Float

When drug stores had soda counters this was one of their most popular drinks. Perhaps too much for today's taste, but as an occasional treat or pick-me-up it is hard to beat.

INGREDIENTS
300ml (½ pint) milk

2 heaped tbsp malted drink powder

2 heaped tbsp drinking chocolate

4 heaped tbsp chocolate or vanilla ice cream

2 scoops chocolate ice cream

Whizz together in a blender the milk, malted drink powder, drinking chocolate and 4 tablespoons of ice cream. Divide the mixture between two tall glasses and serve with a scoop of chocolate ice cream floating in each one.

Makes
2 servings

Iced Chocolate

Use this recipe to make Café Liègeois: add a scoop of vanilla or chocolate ice cream to the Iced Chocolate and top with whipped cream and a sprinkling of cinnamon or cocoa.

INGREDIENTS
250g (8oz) granulated sugar

300ml (½ pint) water

60g (2oz) cocoa powder

2 tsp instant espresso coffee powder

1.25 litres (2 pints) milk

1 Dissolve the sugar in the water over low heat, then bring to the boil and boil briskly for 3 minutes. Whisk in the cocoa and coffee powders.

2 Leave to cool, then chill in the refrigerator until ready to serve.

3 Pour 50–90ml (2–3 fl oz) of the syrup into a glass and top up with milk. Serve in chilled glasses with ice cubes.

Makes
4–6 servings

COFFEE WITH CHOCOLATE

The affinity that chocolate has with coffee is well known. Chocolates served with after-dinner coffee are irresistible. A sprinkling of chocolate or cocoa over the milky froth of a cappuccino adds richness. A pinch of cocoa added to ground coffee, in whatever coffee maker you use, will enhance its flavour. And for a special after-dinner treat add a small square of chocolate to a heated cup, top with hot fresh coffee, add a teaspoon of brandy and float a thin layer of cream over the top of the cup. Serve without stirring.

A small fan of chocolate, set in the whipped cream, is a final touch of luxury

Viennese Hot Chocolate *is a wonderfully warming mixture of rich plain chocolate, cream and milk, with a wicked dash of liqueur.*

The scoop of ice cream on top gives the Chocolate Float its name

Chocolate Float, *once a soda fountain special, is a splendidly cool way to drink chocolate.*

Montezuma

This is a fine drink for sipping after dinner on a summer evening, perhaps outside.

INGREDIENTS

600ml (1pint) milk

1 tbsp granulated sugar

90g (3oz) continental plain chocolate

⅛ tsp cinnamon

⅛ tsp allspice

5 tbsp rum

90ml (3fl oz) brandy or calvados

grated rind of ½ lemon

cracked ice

1 Gently heat the milk, sugar, chocolate, cinnamon and allspice together, and stir continuously until blended. Remove from the heat and leave to cool.

2 Transfer the milk mixture into a cocktail shaker, add the other ingredients and shake. Pour into 4 glasses and serve very cold.

Makes
4 cocktails

Brandy Alexander

Crème de cacao, a popular chocolate-flavoured liqueur, is used for many exotic cocktails. Those that include cream are best served after a meal or at a Christmas gathering in place of egg nog.

INGREDIENTS

ice cubes

125ml (4fl oz) brandy

125ml (4fl oz) crème de cacao

125ml (4fl oz) double cream

freshly grated nutmeg

Put the ice cubes, brandy, crème de cacao and double cream in a cocktail shaker. Shake well, then strain into four cocktail glasses. Grate nutmeg over the top of each and serve immediately.

VARIATIONS
Nureyev
Equal quantities of: vodka and colourless crème de cacao.
Pavlova
Equal quantities of: vodka, crème de cacao and cream.
Pushkin
Equal quantities of: vodka, gin and crème de cacao.
Crow
Equal quantities of: whisky or bourbon and crème de cacao, and a dash of orange bitters.

Makes
4 cocktails

Crow includes whisky and crème de cacao

Nureyev has a Russian touch

Addresses

Squires Kitchen,
3 Waverley Lane,
Farnham, Surrey GU9 8BB
Tel: 01252 711749
Sweet-making and baking equipment; many kinds of chocolate including couverture and modelling paste. Mail order service.

The Chocolate Society,
Clay Pit Lane, Roecliffe,
near Boroughbridge,
North Yorks. YO5 9LS
Tel: 01423 322230
Fine chocolate and materials needed for working with chocolate. Mail order service. The society also has a shop at 36 Elizabeth Street, London SW1W 9NZ
Tel: 0171 259 9222

Corteil and Barratt,
40 High Street,
Ewell Village, Surrey KT17 1RW
Tel: 0181 393 0032
Most kinds of chocolate; baking, cake-decorating and sweet-making equipment. Mail order service.

Sugarworks,
13 Comberton Hill, Kidderminster,
Worcs. DY10 1QG
Tel: 01562 829639
Couverture chocolate to order; chocolate moulds, sweet boxes and cake boards. Mail order service.

Harrods Ltd.,
Knightsbridge, London SW1
Tel: 0171 730 1234
Large chocolate department within the store's famous Food Halls.

Selfridges Ltd.,
400 Oxford Street, London W1 1AB
Tel: 0171 629 1234
Good quality cooking and dessert chocolate, both English and Continental. Cookware department sells baking equipment.

B.R. Mathews and Sons,
12 Gipsy Hill, Crystal Palace,
London SE19 1NN
Tel: 0181 670 0788
Cake-decorating and confectionery-making equipment; some chocolates, including couverture and chocolate drops. Mail order leaflet available.

Divertimenti,
45–47 Wigmore Street,
London W1H 9LE
Tel: 0171 935 0689

and
139–141 Fulham Road,
London SW3 6DS
Tel: 0171 531 8065
Two shops selling cake-decorating, kitchen and baking equipment, chocolate moulds and good quality chocolate. Mail order service (telephone 0171 386 9911 for catalogue).

The Souvenir and Decorations Co.,
Soudeco House, 1a Aldenham Road,
Watford, Herts. WD1 4AD
Tel: 01923 817227
Packaging for confectionery, wedding favours, etc., including bags, ribbons and boxes.

Acknowledgments

Author's Appreciation
I would like to thank the many people at Dorling Kindersley who have been responsible for producing this book, particularly Editorial Director Daphne Razazan, Managing Editor Fay Franklin and the talented art editor Jane Bull. I give my special thanks to my editor, Janice Anderson, for the careful and excellent work she has done on the text. Thanks to photographer Ian O'Leary and his assistant Emma Brogi for the mouthwatering photographs. Janice Murfitt produced and styled all the recipes for the photographs and I am greatly indebted to her for her fine and beautiful work. Many thanks to Zoë Keen and Bryony Miller who helped me work on and test the recipes, Josceline Dimbleby for allowing me to use her Passion Fruit Bombe, and my good friend Nancy Lassalle for her help and the generous use of her kitchen in Cape Cod. Thanks also to my family for all their tasting and useful comments and to John Lowenthal for his measured advice and constant support.

Dorling Kindersley would like to thank Virginia Walter for design management, Paul Wood and Suzy Dittmar for DTP design, Julia Pemberton Hellums for editorial work and Susan Bosanko for the index. Props were supplied by Tables Laid, China & Co., and Surfaces.

Picture Credits
Key to pictures: t = top, c = centre, b = bottom, l = left, r = right.
The publisher would like to thank the following for their kind permission to reproduce the following photographs: Jean-Loup Charmet, Paris 6; Musée de Versailles/E. T. Archive 7; RBG Kew 8; Mary Evans Picture Library 9.
Photography by Ian O'Leary, except:
Dave King 39, 42 br, 43 br, 45 br, 46 r, c, br, 48 ct, b, rt, rb, 51 c, bl, br, 82-3 bl, c, br; David Murray 32r.

040-847-1